Abbreviations

A.A.	anti-aircraft
A/S	anti-submarine
ATW	ahead throwing weapon
B.H.P.	brake horse power
cal	calibre
cyl.	cylinder(s), cylindrical
d.	depth of hull
DC	depth charge
DCH	depth charge howitzer
DCR	depth charge rack
DCT	director control tower
D/F	direction finder
D.P.	dual-purpose
DR.	double reduction
HF/DF	high frequency direction finder
I.H.P.	indicated horse power
k.	knots
LL	electrical sweep
MF/DF	medium frequency direction finder
M.G.	machine gun
m	miles
(oa)	overall length
O.F.	oil fuel
(pp)	perpendicular length
RDF	radar
AW	air warning
GW	general warning (combined air and surface)
SW	surface warning
r.p.m.	revolutions per minute
S.E.	single-ended
S.H.P.	shaft horse power
SR	single reduction
VC	vertical compound
VTE	vertical triple expansion
VQE	vertical quadruple expansion
(wl)	waterline length
I.J.N.	Imperial Japanese Navy
R.B.N.	Royal Belgian Navy
R.C.N.	Royal Canadian Navy
R.E.N.	Royal Egyptian Navy
R.H.N.	Royal Hellenic Navy
R.N.N.	Royal Norwegian Navy
R.Neth.N.	Royal Netherlands Navy
R.Th.N.	Royal Thai Navy
R.N.	Royal Navy
U.S.N.	United States Navy
U.S.C.G.	United States Coast Guard
U.S.C. & G.S.	United States Coast & Geodetic Survey

Note 1: The United States Navy retained the term gunboat for a vessel which was generally classed as a sloop or escort vessel in other navies.

Note 2: These vessels are fully detailed in the two companion volumes on *American Fleet & Escort Destroyers.*

Note 3: See *British Escort Ships.*

Bicester 1974   H.T.L.

Foreword

The escort and minesweeping forces o. ... .erably below strength in 1939 and composed of a motley collection of gunboats (see *Note 1*) and a small number of elderly minesweepers. There was also a substantial reserve—of old destroyers, and the large and medium cutters of the United States Coast Guard, which could also be utilised for the protection of Trade. The origins of this situation lay in the American policy of isolation which gained strength in the period "between the wars" and held that the U.S.A. should hold aloof from foreign—particularly European —entanglements. In pursuance of this policy the United States Navy's paramount duty was the defence of American territories, and despite long lines of communications in the Pacific the requirements for Trade protection for a country rich in natural resources had low priority.

The naval strategy of the U.S.A. centred around operating and supporting its main fleet in the Pacific, with Japan as the potential enemy in mind, and the build-up of the combatant strength of the Pacific Fleet had overriding priority. In this atmosphere there was an understandable tendency for the supply of such vessels as escorts and mine-sweepers to be deferred in favour of fleet vessels.

It is, perhaps, no over-simplification to say that the Pacific Fleet's principal task was the defence of the Philippine Islands, which were ideally located as a forward base for operations against Japan; and without doubt the fleet stood as the principal bulwark against Japanese aggression in East and South-East Asia.

Although two prototype minesweepers (AM.55 and 56) were authorised in 1938, no other provision than twelve more minesweepers (AM.57–68) had been put in hand by 1940. Under the terms of Lend/Lease the United States Navy was able to spare fifty old destroyers for transfer to the hard-pressed Royal Navy, but could only meet requests for escorts and minesweepers by new construction. The former had first to be designed to meet broad British requirements but also to suit American practice as to construction and equipment in order to expedite delivery, and the result was the sturdy destroyer escort (DE); while the new American standard minesweeper ("Auk" class) served British requirements equally as well.

When finally drawn into the Second World War the circumstances could hardly have been less favourable to the U.S.A. First, the Pacific Fleet was put out of action by the treacherous Japanese naval air strike on Pearl Harbour; second, with the Pacific Fleet immobilised the Japanese swept through and occupied South-East Asia (including the Philippines); and third, the U.S.A. was now committed to supply vast quantities of war supplies to her Allies over practically undefended trade routes. It is a matter of history that unsurpassed American war production eventually met all demands, but in the interim a high rate of loss was sustained by the Allied merchant fleets.

So acute was the initial shortage of escorts and minesweepers that even prior to the American entry into war the United States Navy was compelled to requisition fishing vessels and yachts to serve as armed auxiliaries in these roles; and early in 1942 even the Royal Navy—whose resources were stretched to the limit—had to lend the United States Navy ten corvettes and twenty-two A/S trawlers. The DE design (see *Note 2*) drawn-up for the Royal Navy was wholly acceptable to the United States Navy. Put into large-scale production, this design provided for the bulk of American escort forces. Therefore, excluding the destroyer escort, only a relatively modest provision (100 frigates) was made for further escorts under the war programmes. Minesweeper construction, on the other hand, was on a large scale. To speed production and meet numerical requirements unit size was reduced to the minimum level, while to counter sophisticated influence mines a wood-hulled sweeper—the ubiquitous YMS—was later introduced and proved an outstanding success.

Listed in these volumes are all the regular and auxiliary escort and fleet minesweepers of the United States Navy during the Second World War. It was decided to include the auxiliaries as they were numbered consecutively with the regular units in their various categories, and in order to conserve space only brief particulars are provided for those vessels of British design (some corvettes, frigates, and minesweepers) which have already been listed in full detail in companion volumes (see *Note 3*). In addition, it was appreciated that considerable interest centred around auxiliary warships in general, and all too often they are only reported on briefly, or omitted altogether. Within the time span allotted to this book every effort has been made to secure fate details, but in many instances it has not been possible to determine whether a vessel was scrapped or passed into mercantile ownership after it had been sold-out of naval service.

Particular acknowledgements are due to the information and photographic services of the United States Navy whose ready assistance was much appreciated; and to many colleagues in the U.K. and the U.S.A. who were no less helpful.

Gunboats

The five old gunboats in service at the outbreak of the Second World War were wholly obsolete but their retention underlined the extreme shortage of escort and patrol vessels. In 1938 the *Asheville* and *Tulsa* were refitted when their tall and thin funnels were reduced in height, and the *Sacramento* was similarly altered when converted to oil-firing, but the older *Dubuque* and *Paducah* remained coal-fired and kept their tall natural-draught funnels. They were all too old and slow for active employment, and after some initial patrol work were otherwise mainly used for training. In 1943 the *Dubuque* was re-armed with three 5in (3 × 1) guns which better suited her training role, and had her two funnels trunked into a single uptake.

Below: The gunboat TULSA *before refitting. Bottom: The* SACRAMENTO.   PHOTOGRAPHS: U.S. NAVY

Gunboats: **DUBUQUE, PADUCAH**
990 tons: 173(wl) 200½(oa) × 35 × 12¼ *feet:* two Babcock & Wilcox boilers, two shafts, reciprocating (VTE) I.H.P. 1,000 = 12 knots, coal: one 5-inch, two 4-inch (2 × 1), one 3-inch A.A. guns: complement 170.

Gunboat: **SACRAMENTO**
1,025 tons: 210(wl) 226¼(oa) × 40¾ × 9½ feet: two Babcock & Wilcox boilers, one shaft, reciprocating (VTE) I.H.P. 950 = 12 knots, oil fuel: two 4-inch (2 × 1), one 3-inch A.A. guns: complement 153.

Gunboats: **ASHEVILLE, TULSA**
1,200 tons (1,760 tons full load): 225(wl) 241¼(oa) × 41¼ × 10 feet: three modified Thornycroft boilers, two shafts, Parsons geared turbines S.H.P. 1,200 = 12 knots, O.F. 440 tons: three 4-inch (3 × 1), one 3-inch A.A. guns: complement 175.

Dubuque *Hull No:* PG.17	*Built by:* Gas Engine & Power and Charles L. Seabury (Morris Heights)
Launched: 15.8.04	Sold 1.47.
Paducah *Hull No:* PG.18	*Built by:* As above
Launched: 11.10.04	Sold Maria Angelo (Miami) 19.12.46.
Sacramento *Hull No:* PG.19	*Build by:* Cramp (Philadephia)
Launched: 21.2.14	Mercantile *Fermina* (1947).
Asheville *Hull No:* PG.21	*Built by:* Charleston N.Y.
Launched: 4.7.18	Gunfire I.J.N. cruisers and destroyers south of Java 3.3.42.
Tulsa *Hull No:* PG.22	*Built by:* As above
Launched: 25.8.22	*Tacloban* (1944); sold 10.46.

Machinery contracts: Engined by builders.

"Erie" class:
Charleston, Erie

This class was designed to act as ocean escorts, but generally proved unsatisfactory more on the grounds of the unrealistic requirements framed by the General Board rather than by design interpretation, which amply met the conditions laid down. It was arbitrarily decided to go to the upper limits permitted by the London Naval Treaty.in displacement (2,000 tons), speed (20 knots), and armament (four 6in guns) for vessels of this type rather than examine if these parameters combined to meet a tactical need.

In shipping the heaviest permitted armament of four 6in guns the emphasis was directed more to surface action than the more essential A.A. and A/S qualities required by an escort. The 6in guns were arranged in open shields and were conventionally disposed two forward and two aft with the inner guns superimposed. Unlike any other contemporary sloop some measure of protection was provided with an armoured main deck and thin side armour around the machinery spaces, armoured crowns to the magazines, a 3in conning tower, and 1in gunshields. A DCT for controlling the 6in guns was mounted over the conning tower. As most mercantile raiders were envisaged as 16-knot vessels carrying six/eight 6in guns the margin of superiority possessed by the *Erie* in gunpower and speed was too fine to be decisive. The A.A. armament comprised four quadruple heavy MG.s disposed on the centreline forward and aft and in the bridge wings, while a seaplane was accommodated on a platform abaft the funnel.

DISPLACEMENT: 2,000 tons (2,715 tons full load).

DIMENSIONS: 308(wl) 328½(oa) × 41¼ × 12¾ (14¾ full load) feet.

MACHINERY: Two Babcock & Wilcox boilers; two shafts; Parsons SR geared turbines S.H.P. 6,200 = 20 knots.

BUNKERS AND RADIUS: O.F. 570 tons; 8,000/4,000 miles @ 12½/20 knots.

PROTECTION: Main belt (amid) 1 inch, main deck (amid) 1¼ inches, magazine crowns 3 inches. C.T. 3 inches, gunshields 1 inch.

ARMAMENT: Four 6-inch/47cal (4 × 1), sixteen 1·1-inch A.A. (4 × 4) guns; one aircraft.

COMPLEMENT: 190 (231 as flag/240 war).

Pre-war view of the gunboat ERIE *showing derricks for aircraft and boats amidships, and high after superstructure. Note DCT for 6in guns on top of enclosed bridge and, although no aircraft is carried, provision was made to stow one abaft the funnel.* PHOTOGRAPH: IWM

The hull was flush-decked and oddly adopted the outmoded clipper stem and counter stern which gave them a distinctive—but dated—appearance. Rigging comprised a tripod foremast, while derricks were stepped from the tall after structure for handling the aircraft and boats. Fairly extensive flag accommodation was provided primarily to suit their peace-time employment. When completed they were the most powerful sloops of their day, and were only approached by the Dutch *Van Kinsbergen* (1,700 tons, 25½ knots, four 4·7in guns), the Portuguese "Afonso de Albuquerque" class (1,810 tons, 21 knots, four 4·7in and two 3in A.A. guns, one aircraft), and the Thai "Tachin" class (1,400 tons, 17 knots, four 4·7in guns and four 21in T.T.).

The loss of the *Erie* proved a protracted affair. After being torpedoed by a German submarine off Curacao she was beached and gutted by fire. She was later re-floated and towed to Willemstadt where she subsequently capsized. In 1952 the *Erie* was again salved and scuttled in deep water off Curacao. War modifications were only extended to the *Charleston* when the aircraft and derricks were removed and replaced by six 20mm A.A. (6 × 1) guns, SR.RDF was fitted to the DCT, and SW.RDF added on the foremast.

Although no more units of this type were built the design experience was utilised by the United States Coast Guard for the large cutters of the "Hamilton" class. On basically the same hull the superstructure was modified and reduced, all armour was omitted, and the 6in were replaced by 5in guns. Paradoxically, because they so successfully met Coast Guard requirements the "Hamilton" class enjoyed a high reputation, which highlighted the prime failing of the *Erie*: a well-designed ship which afforded the type of trade protection that was best provided by the larger cruiser.

Erie	*Built by:* New York N.Y.
Hull No: PG.50	
	Torpedoed German
Launched:	submarine *U.163*
29.2.36	Caribbean 12.11.42 and
	subsequently capsized
	Willemstadt 5.12.42.

Charleston	*Built by:* Charleston N.Y.
Hull No: PG.51	
	Sold Massachusetts
Launched:	Marine Academy 25/3/48.
26.2.36	

Machinery contracts: Engined by builders.

The CHARLESTON *(4 Mar 1944) showing war modifications: RDF has been fitted at the head of the foremast and on the DCT, six 20mm A.A. (6× 1) A.A. guns added, and racks provided at the stern for DCs. Note prominent bandstands on which 'A' and 'Y' guns are mounted.* PHOTOGRAPH: U.S. NAVY

Auxiliary Gunboats and Armed Yachts

These vessels were acquired in 1940–41 and were armed and fitted-out for escort and patrol work, and clearly illustrated the emergency measures taken by the United States Navy to cope with the deficiency in escorts. The larger units were classed as gunboats (PG), and the remainder as either sea-going (PY) or coastal (PYc) armed yachts; but between 1942–44 most were relegated to training and subsidiary services as war-built escorts became available.

Three units—the *Niagara*, *Hilo*, and *Jamestown*—were converted to MTB tenders (AGP.1–3); the *Nourmahal* was transferred to the United States Coast Guard in 1943; the *Jade* (later replaced by the *Turquoise*) was loaned to Venezuela; and the *Natchez*, acquired from the United States Coast & Geodetic Survey, was never placed in service as a gunboat but continued as a surveying vessel. The *Niagara* was first acquired for conversion to a coastal minelayer (CMo.2) but this was not implemented.

Most auxiliary gunboats were armed with one/two 3in A.A. guns, sonar, and depth charges; and only a few later received such refinements as 20mm A.A. guns and RDF. However, these units were never intended to be other than a stop-gap measure, and were taken out of active employment as soon as circumstances permitted.

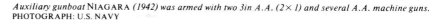

Auxiliary gunboat NIAGARA *(1942) was armed with two 3in A.A. (2×1) and several A.A. machine guns.*
PHOTOGRAPH: U.S. NAVY

Niagara
(ex-yacht
H-Esmaro)
Hull No : PG.52

Completed :
8.29

Built by : Bath I.W.

AGP.1 (1943).

St. Augustine
(ex-yacht *No
Paro, Viking*)
Hull No : PG.54

Completed :
1929

Built by : Newport News

Collision mercantile
Camas Meadows off Cape
May 6.1.44.

Williamsburg
(ex-yacht *Aras*)
Hull No : PG.56

Completed :
1.31

Built by : Bath I.W.

AGC.369 (1946),
mercantile *Anton Bruun*
(1963); hulked 1969.

Vixen
(ex-yacht *Orion*)
Hull No : PG.53

Completed :
8.29

Built by : Germaniawerft
(Kiel)

Yacht *Vixen* (1947).

Jamestown
(ex-yacht *Alder*,
ex-*Savannah*)
Hull No : PG.55

Completed :
1.28

Built by : Pusey & Jones
(Wilmington)

AGP.3 (1943).

Plymouth
(ex-yacht *Alva*)
Hull No : PG.57

Completed :
3.31

Built by : Germaniawerft
(Kiel)

Torpedoed German
submarine *U.566* off North
Carolina 5.8.43.

Auxiliary gunboat VIXEN *(11 Apr 1944) was armed with two 3in A.A. (2× 1) and eight heavy (8× 1) A.A.
machine guns.* PHOTOGRAPH: U.S. NAVY

Auxiliary gunboat ST. AUGUSTINE *(22 May 1943) was armed with three 3in A.A. (3× 1) and four heavy
(4× 1) A.A. machine guns, and fitted with SW.RDF at the head of the foremast.*
PHOTOGRAPH: U.S. NAVY

Hilo
(ex-yacht *Moana*,
ex-*Caroline*)
Hull No : PG.58

Completed :
9.31

Built by : Bath I.W.

AGP.2 (1943).

San Bernardino
(ex-yacht
Vanda)
Hull No : PG.59

Completed :
11.28

Built by : As above

Yacht *Vanda* (1946):
sold 1969 and
scrapped.

Beaumont
(ex-yacht *Carola*,
ex-*Chalena*,
ex-*Reveler*)
Hull No : PG.60

Completed :
10.30

Built by : Germaniawerft
(Kiel)

Yacht *Elpetal* (1947).

Dauntless
(ex-yacht
Delphine)
Hull No : PG.61

Completed :
3.21

Built by : Great Lakes Eng.
(Ecorse)

Yacht *Delphine* (1947).

Nourmahal
(ex-yacht
Nourmahal)
Hull No : PG.72

Completed :
6.28

Built by : Germaniawerft
(Kiel)

U.S.C.G. (name
unchanged—1944).

Natchez(i)
(ex-USC & GS
Oceanographer,
ex-USN *Corsair*,
ex-yacht *Corsair*)
Hull No : PG.85

Completed :
1898

Built by : W. & A. Fletcher
(Hoboken)

Oceanographer
(AGS.2—1942).

Ex-yacht: **NIAGARA**
1,022 tons: 215(wl) 267(oa) × 25½ × 22½d/14½ feet: two shafts, 8-cyl. Cooper-Bessemer diesel engines (bore 18″ × 22″) stroke) B.H.P. 3,000 = 16 knots, oil fuel: two 3-inch A.A. (2 × 1) guns: complement 139.

Ex-yacht: **VIXEN**
3,060 tons: 305(wl) 332½(oa) × 46¾ × 23½d/16 feet: two shafts, 8-cyl. Krupp diesel engines (bore 550mm × 900mm stroke) B.H.P. 3,600 = 17 knots, oil fuel: two 3-inch A.A. (2 × 1) guns: complement not known.

Ex-yacht: **ST. AUGUSTINE**
1,975 tons: 217½(pp) 272(oa) × 15¾/13 feet: two boilers, shafts, General Electric turbines and electric motors S.H.P. 2,600 = 16 knots, oil fuel: three 3-inch A.A. (3 × 1), four ·5-inch A.A. (4 × 1) guns: complement not known.

Ex-yacht **JAMESTOWN**
1,780 tons: 280(wl) 294(oa) × 38¼ × 22d/16 feet: two shafts, 8-cyl. Cooper-Bessemer diesel engines (bore 18″ × 22″ stroke) B.H.P. 3,000 = 15 knots, oil fuel: two 3-inch A.A. (2 × 1) guns: complement 259.

Ex-yacht: **WILLIAMSBURG**
1,730 tons: 227½(wl) 243¾(oa) × 36 × 19d/15 feet: two shafts, 8-cyl. Winton diesel engines (bore 17″ × 26″ stroke) B.H.P. 2,200 = 16 knots, oil fuel: one 3-inch A.A. gun: complement not known.

Ex-yacht: **PLYMOUTH**
1,500 tons: 259¼(wl) 264½(oa) × 46¼ × 25d/18 feet: two shafts, 8-cyl. Krupp diesel engine (bore 600mm × 1050mm stroke) B.H.P. 4,200 = 15 knots, oil fuel: one 4-inch, A.A. (4 × 1), four ·5-inch A.A. (4 × 1) guns: complement 155.

Ex-yacht: **HILO**
2,350 tons: 235½(pp) 279(oa) × 38¼ × 22¾d/17 feet: two shafts, 8-cyl. Cooper-Bessemer diesel engines (bore 18″ × 22″ stroke) B.H.P. 3,000 = 17 knots, oil fuel: one 3-inch A.A. gun: complement 116.

Ex-yacht: **SAN BERNARDINO**
1,500 tons: 220(wl) 240(oa) × 37 × 20d/14½ feet: two shafts, 8-cyl. Cooper-Bessemer diesel engines (bore 18″ × 22″ stroke) B.H.P. 3,000 = 16 knots, oil fuel: two 3-inch A.A. (2 × 1) guns: complement not known.

Ex-yacht: **BEAUMONT**
1,434 tons: 206(wl) 247½(oa) × 34 × 17d/12½ feet: two shafts, 8-cyl. Krupp diesel engines (bore 400mm × 670mm stroke) B.H.P. 1,800 = 15½ knots, oil fuel: two 3-inch A.A. (2 × 1) guns: complement 110.

Ex-yacht: **DAUNTLESS**
1,950 tons: 250½(wl) 257¾(oa) × 35½ × 17¼d/14¾ feet: three w.t. boilers (250lb/in²), two shafts, reciprocating (VQE—cyl. 14½″: 21″: 30½″: 45″ × 30″ stroke) I.H.P. 2,900 = 16 knots, oil fuel: two 3-inch A.A. (2 × 1) guns: complement 135.

Ex-yacht: **NOURMAHAL**
2,250 tons: 260(wl) 263¾(oa) × 41½ × 22d/16¾ feet: two shafts, 6-cyl. Sulzer diesel engines (bore 470mm × 790mm stroke) B.H.P. 2,400 = 15 knots, oil fuel: two 4-inch (2 × 1) guns: complement 153.

Ex-mercantile: **NATCHEZ**
Not placed in service as gunboat.

Machinery contracts: Niagara, Jamestown, Hilo, and *San Bernardino* engined by Cooper-Bessemer; *Vixen, Plymouth,* and *Beamont* by Fried. Krupp; *St. Augustine* by General Electric; *Williamsburg* by Winto; *Nourmahal* by Sulzer; and *Dauntless* by builders.

The PLYMOUTH *(1 May 1942) was the most heavily-armed auxiliary gunboat with one 4in and four 3in A.A. (4 × 1) guns, and had a pedestal director on the bridge.* PHOTOGRAPH: U.S. NAVY

Auxiliary gunboat DAUNTLESS *(below) and* JAMESON *(bottom). The former was armed with two 3in A.A. (2 × 1) and four heavy A.A. (4 × 1) machine guns, while the latter has been dis-armed.* PHOTOGRAPHS: U.S. NAVY

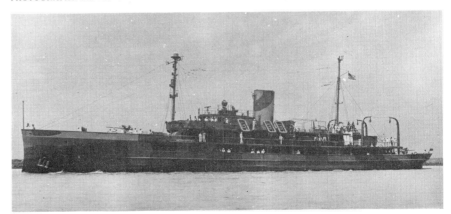

"Flower" class: Courage, Fury, Impulse, Ready, Restless, Saucy, Spry, Surprise, Temptress, Tenacity

898 tons (1,180 tons full load): 190(pp) 205¼(oa) × 33¼ × 10¼ (12¾ full load) feet: two SE cylindrical boilers (225lb/in²), one shaft, reciprocating (VTE—cyl. 18½″:31″:38½″(2) × 30″ stroke) I.H.P. 2,750 = 16 knots, O.F. 232 tons (4,500m @ 10k): one 4-inch, one 3-inch A.A., two/four 20mm A.A. (2/4 × 1) guns: complement 89.

No sooner was the U.S.A. at war than a determined onslaught was made by German submarines on the American Atlantic seaboard, which was used both by coastal shipping and deep-sea vessels en-route to, and from, terminal points for ocean convoys. As the area was vital and losses high, even the hard-pressed Royal Navy was compelled to assist the United States Navy and loaned ten "Flower" class corvettes and twenty-two A/S trawlers early in 1942.

As they came up for refit the corvettes were modified by shipping American guns: generally, the British 4in forward was replaced by an American gun of the same calibre, or by a 3in A.A. in some, and the 2pdr A.A. aft by a 3in A.A. gun; two/four 20mm A.A. (2/4 × 1) guns were added, and the British SW.RDF on the bridge by an American set fitted on the foremast. Later modifications included replacing the pole mast forward of the bridge by a tripod abaft the bridge, and the addition of a spigot A/S mortar (Hedgehog).

These vessels were retained by the United States Navy up to the end of the war, which was somewhat surprising in the view of the large number of escorts later available under war construction. When returned to the Royal Navy the *Saucy* was renamed *Snapdragon* as her original name had been awarded to another British corvette.

The IMPULSE *(27 Jul 1942) was an ex-British corvette and has been re-armed with a 4in gun forward and a 3in A.A. gun aft, but still has British SW.RDF on the bridge.* PHOTOGRAPH: U.S. NAVY

Quarter view of the TEMPTRESS *(19 Oct 1943) showing four A/S mortars and two stern racks for forty-four deck-stowed depth charges.* PHOTOGRAPH: U.S. NAVY

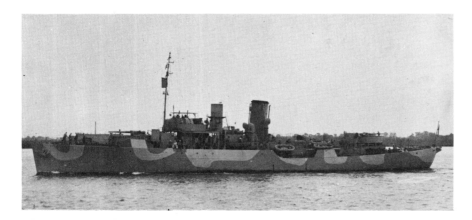

Temptress (ex-RN *Veronica*) Hull No: PG.62	Returned R.N. 1945.	**Ready** (ex-RN *Calendula*) Hull No: PG.67	Returned R.N. 1945.
Surprise (ex-RN *Heliotrope*) Hull No: PG.63	Returned R.N. 1945.	**Impulse** (ex-RN *Begonia*) Hull No: PG.68	Returned R.N. 1945.
Spry (ex-RN *Hibiscus*) Hull No: PG.65	Returned R.N. 1945.	**Fury** (ex-RN *Larkspur*) Hull No: PG.69	Returned R.N. 23.8.45.
Saucy (ex-RN *Arabis*) Hull PG.65	R.N. *Snapdragon* (1945)	**Courage** (ex-RN *Heartsease*, ex-*Pansy*) Hull No: PG.70	Returned R.N. 23.8.45.
Restless (ex-RN *Periwinkle*) Hull No: PG.66	Returned R.N. 1945.	**Tenacity** (ex-RN *Candytuft*) Hull No: PG.71	Returned R.N. .....45.

Bow view of the SURPRISE *(19 May 1944) showing modified rig: a light tripod stepped abaft the bridge has replaced the pole foremast, and two more 20mm A.A. (2 × 1) guns have been added at the break of the fo'c's'le.*
PHOTOGRAPH: U.S. NAVY

Modified "Flower" class:

Action, Alacrity, Beacon, Brisk, Caprice, Clash, Haste, Intensity, Might, Pert, Prudent, Splendor, Tact, Vim, Vitality.

These vessels were first ordered for transfer to the Royal Navy under Lend/Lease, but owing to the extreme shortage of escorts the United States Navy retained eight so that only seven were finally turned over. They were built to the modified "Flower" design which incorporated many minor improvements war experience had shown desirable, and principally differed from their British counterparts by shipping two American pattern 3in A.A. guns forward and aft.

976 tons (1,248 tons full load): 193(pp) 208¼(oa) × 33¼ × 11 (14 full load) feet: two Admiralty 3-drum boilers (225lb/in²), one shaft, reciprocating (VTE—cyl. 18½″ : 31″ : 38½″ (2) × 30″ stroke) I.H.P. 2,750 = 16 knots, O.F. 340 tons (7,000m @ 10k): two 3-inch A.A. (2 × 1), four 20mm A.A. (4 × 1) guns, one A/S spigot mortar (Hedgehog): complement 89.

Action
Hull No: PG.86
R.N. *Comfrey* (1942), U.S.N. *Action* (1942).

Alacrity
Hull No: PG.87
R.N. *Cornel* (1942), U.S.N. *Alacrity* (1942).

Beacon
Hull No: PG.88
R.N. *Dittany* (1942); returned U.S.N. 20.6.46.

Brisk
Hull No: PG.89
R.N. *Flax* (1942), U.S.N. *Brisk* (1942).

Caprice
Hull No: PG.90
R.N. *Honesty* (1943); returned U.S.N. 5.1.46.

Clash
Hull No: PG.91
R.N. *Linaria* (1943); returned U.S.N. 27.7.46.

Haste
Hull No: PG.92
R.N. *Mandrake* (1942), U.S.N. *Haste* (1942).

Intensity
Hull No: PG.93
R.N. *Milfoil* (1942), U.S.N. *Intensity* (1942).

Might
Hull No: PG.94
R.N. *Musk* (1942), U.S.N. *Might* (1942).

Pert
Hull No: PG.95
R.N. *Nepeta* (1942), U.S.N. *Pert* (1943).

Prudent
Hull No: PG.96
R.N. *Privet* (1942), U.S.N. *Prudent* (1942).

Splendor
Hull No: PG.97
R.N. *Rosebay* (1943); returned U.S.N. 20.3.46.

Tact
Hull No: PG.98
R.N. *Smilax* (1943); returned U.S.N. 20.3.46.

Vim
Hull No: PG.99
R.N. *Statice* (1943); returned U.S.N. 21.6.46.

Vitality
Hull No: PG.100
R.N. *Willowherb* (1943); returned U.S.N. 11.6.46.

The British RDF on the bridge has been replaced by an American set at the masthead in the PRUDENT *(6 Apr 1954). Note additional depth charge stowage racks at the stern.* PHOTOGRAPH: U.S. NAVY

Right: The Canadian-built HASTE *(6 Sep 1943) (top) incorporated many war modifications. The* INTENSITY *(7 Sep 1943) (below) shipped 3in A.A. guns forward and aft, with the forward gun on a raised platform that also accommodated the Hedgehog A/S mortar (to starboard).*
PHOTOGRAPHS: U.S. NAVY

"River" class:

Asheville, Natchez, and Eight units for the Royal Navy.

As with the corvettes these frigates were first ordered for transfer to the Royal Navy under Lend/Lease, but only two were retained for type evaluation by the United States Navy and the remaining eight were turned over. The two American units carried a heavier armament than their British counterparts and shipped 3in A.A. instead of 4in guns but with the addition of a third gun on the fo'c'sle, two twin 40mm A.A. mountings were positioned at the break of the long fo'c'sle together with their RDF-fitted directors, four 20mm A.A. guns were grouped around the bridge, and an A/S spigot mortar (Hedgehog) was fitted abaft the fo'c'sle 3in gun. These vessels were first classed as gunboats (PG) but subsequently introduced the new category of frigate (PF). The *Asheville* was sold to the Argentinian Navy in 1946 and renamed *Hercules*, and was again renamed *Juan B. Azopardo* on transfer to the Coast Guard in 1963; while the *Natchez* was sold to the Dominican Navy in 1948 and renamed *Juan Pablo Duarte* and passed into mercantile ownership as the *Moineau* in 1957.

1,418 tons (2,160 tons full load): 283(pp) 301¼(oa) × 36½ × 7(12¾ full load) feet: two Admiralty 3-drum boilers (225lb/in²), two shafts, reciprocating (VTE—cyl. 18½″: 31″: 38½″(2) × 30″ stroke) I.H.P. 5,500 = 20 knots, O.F. 650 tons: three 3-inch/50cal A.A. (3 × 1), four 40mm A.A. (2 × 2), four 20mm A.A. (4 × 1) guns, one A/S spigot mortar (Hedgehog): complement 180 (war 194).

Unnamed Hull No: PG.101	R.N. *Adur* (1942), U.S.N. *Asheville (ii)* (1942), PF.1 (1943).	Unnamed Hull No: PG.106	R.N. *Findhorn* (1942); returned U.S.N. 20.3.46.
Unnamed Hull No: PG.102	R.N. *Annan* (1942), U.S.N. *Natchez (ii)* (1942), PF.2 (1943).	Unnamed Hull No: PG.107	R.N. *Inver* (1942); returned U.S.N. 4.3.46.
Unnamed Hull No: PG.103	R.N. *Barle* (1942); returned U.S.N. 27.2.46.	Unnamed Hull No: PG.108	R.N. *Lossie* (1942); returned U.S.N. 26.1.46.
Unnamed Hull No: PG.104	R.N. *Cuckmere* (1942); torpedoed German *U.223* off Algiers 11.12.43.	Unnamed Hull No: PG.109	R.N. *Parrett* (1942); returned U.S.N. 5.2.46.
Danville Hull No: PG.105	R.N. *Evenlode* (1942); returned U.S.N. 5.3.46.	Unnamed Hull No: PG.110	R.N. *Shiel* (1942); returned U.S.N. 4.3.46.

The Canadian-built NATCHEZ (13 Oct 1943) could be distinguished from her American counterparts by the British SW. RDF on the bridge and the tripod foremast. Note Hedgehog A/S mortar on the fo'c'sle abaft "A" gun.   PHOTOGRAPH: U.S. NAVY

"Tacoma" class:

This class was built to the British "River" design by the United States Navy with slight modifications to incorporate all-welded construction, and they were rigged with only a pole foremast which carried the SW.RDF aerial. Later units had the light A.A. armament increased to nine 20mm A.A. with guns added amidships (2×1) and aft (3×1), and most earlier units were also brought up to this standard. They were originally classed as gunboats (PG.111–210) but were re-rated as frigates (PF) while building. They closely resembled the British frigates in appearance, but could be easily distinguished by their heavier gun armament and pole foremast.

Because of the design's mercantile origins contracts were placed by the Maritime Commission on behalf of the United States Navy, which eased the supervisory load borne by the latter with the vast war building programmes in hand. In view of the large destroyer escort (DE) programme, and the individual superiority of the destroyer escort compared with the frigate (PF), the provision for frigates was relatively modest and only one hundred were ordered. Of these twenty-one were transferred to the Royal Navy under Lend/Lease and four were cancelled, and the balance were turned over to the United States Coast Guard for manning. Towards the close of the war twenty-eight frigates were loaned to the Soviet Navy as part of the military price to secure the U.S.S.R's participation in the planned invasion of Japan.

DISPLACEMENT: 1,430 tons (2,415 tons full load).

DIMENSIONS: $285\frac{1}{2}$(wl) 304(oa) $\times 37\frac{1}{2} \times 8$ ($13\frac{3}{4}$ full load) feet.

MACHINERY: Two Babcock & Wilcox boilers; two shafts; reciprocating (VTE—cyl. $18\frac{1}{2}''$: $31''$: $38\frac{1}{2}''$(2) $\times 30''$ stroke) I.H.P. $5,500 = 20$ knots.

BUNKERS AND RADIUS: O.F. 645 tons; 9,500 miles @ 12 knots.

ARMAMENT: Three 3-inch/50cal A.A. (3×1), four 40mm A.A. (2×2), four (earlier units)/ nine (later units) 20mm A.A. ($4/9 \times 1$) guns; one A/S spigot mortar (Hedgehog).

COMPLEMENT: 180 (214 war).

Tacoma
Hull No: PF.3

Launched:
7.7.43

Built by: Kaiser Cargo (Richmond)

Soviet Navy *EK.12* (1945–49), South Korean Navy *Taedong* (1951).

Sausalito
Hull No: PF.4

Launched:
20.7.43

Built by: As above

Soviet Navy *EK.13* (1945–49), South Korean Navy *Imjin* (1952).

Hoquiam
Hull No: PF.5

Launched:
31.7.43

Built by: As above

Soviet Navy *EK.14* (1945–49), South Korean Navy *Naktong* (1951).

Pasco
Hull No: PF.6

Launched:
17.8.43

Built by: As above

Soviet Navy *EK.15* (1945–49), Japanese M.S.D.F. *Kashi* (1953), hulked (1965); South Korean Navy (1969) and cannibalised.

Albuquerque
Hull No: PF.7

Launched:
14.9.43

Built by: As above

Soviet Navy *EK.16* (1945–49), Japanese M.S.D.F. *Touchi* (1953).

Everett
Hull No: PF.8

Launched:
29.9.43

Built by: As above

Soviet Navy *EK.16* (1945–49), Japanese M.S.D.F. *Kiri* (1953).

Pocatello
Hull No: PF.9

Launched:
17.10.43

Built by: As above

Sold J. C. Berkwit (New York) 9.47 and scrapped.

Brownsville
Hull No: PF.10

Launched:
14.11.43

Built by: As above

Sold 30.9.47 and scrapped.

Grand Forks
Hull No: PF.11

Launched:
27.11.43

Built by: Kaiser Cargo (Richmond)

Sold J. G. Berwick (New York) 19.5.47 and scrapped.

Casper
Hull No: PF.12

Launched:
27.12.43

Built by: As above

Sold 20.5.47 and scrapped.

Pueblo
Hull No: PF.13

Launched:
20.1.44

Built by: As above

Dominican Navy *Presidente Troncoso* (1947), *Gregorio Luperon* (1952).

Grand Island
Hull No: PF.14

Launched:
19.2.44

Built by: As Above

Cuban Navy *Maximo Gomez* (1947).

Key West
Hull No: PF.17

Launched:
29.12.43

Built by: As above

Sold Cascade Enterprises (Oakland) 18.4.47 and scrapped.

Gulfport
Hull No: PF.20

Launched:
21.8.43

Built by: American Sbdg. (Cleveland)

Sold Zīdell Ship Dismantling 13.11.47 and scrapped Seattle.

Annapolis
Hull No: PF.15

Launched:
16.10.43

Built by: American Sbdg. (Lorain)

Mexican Navy *Usumacinta* (1947).

Alexandria
Hull No: PF.18

Launched:
15.1.44

Built by: As above

Sold 18.4.47 and scrapped.

Bayonne
Hull No: PF.21

Launched:
11.9.43

Built by: As above

Soviet Navy *EK.24* (1945–49), Japanese M.S.D.F. *Buna* (1953), hulked (1965).

Bangor
Hull No: PF.16

Launched:
6.11.43

Built by: As above

Mexican Navy *Tehuantepec* (1947).

Huron
Hull No: PF.19

Launched:
3.7.43

Built by: American Sbdg. (Cleveland)

Mercantile *Jose Marcelino* (1948).

Gloucester
Hull No: PF.22

Launched:
12.7.43

Built by: Walter Butler Shyd. (Superior)

Soviet Navy *EK.25* (1945–49), Japanese M.S.D.F. *Tsuge* (1953).

Shreveport
Hull No: PF.23

Launched:
15.7.43

Built by: As above

Sold 1947 and scrapped.

The TACOMA *– lead ship of her class – as completed (10 Dec 1943) (below), and with only the fore part of the upper bridge plated. The light A.A. armament of the* ALBUQUERQUE *(20 May 1944) (bottom) has been augmented by the addition of two 20mm (2 × 1) amidships and three 20mm (3 × 1) guns aft. Both AW and SW.RDF are carried at the masthead.* PHOTOGRAPHS: U.S. NAVY

Muskegon
Hull No: PF.24

Launched:
25.7.43

Built by: As above

French Navy *Mermoz* (1947); sold 1958 and scrapped.

Charlottesville
Hull No: PF.25

Launched:
30.7.43

Built by: As above

Soviet Navy *EK.1* (1945–49), Japanese M.S.D.F. *Maki* (1953), hulked (1966).

Poughkeepsie
Hull No: PF.26

Launched:
12.8.43

Built by: As above

Soviet Navy *EK25* (1945–49), Japanese M.S.D.F. *Momi* (1953), hulked (1965); South Korean Navy (1969) and cannibalised.

Newport
Hull No: PF.27

Launched:
15.8.43

Built by: As above

Soviet Navy *EK.27* (1945–49), Japanese M.S.D.F. *Kaede* (1953), hulked (1966).

Emporia
Hull No: PF.28

Launched:
30.8.43

Built by: As above

French Navy *Le Verrier* (1947); sold 1958 and scrapped.

Groton
Hull No: PF.29

Launched:
14.9.43

Built by: Walter Butler
Shyd. (Superior)

Colombian Navy
Almirante Padilla (1947).

Hingham
Hull No: PF.30

Launched:
27.8.43

Built by: As above

Sold Sun Sbdg. & D.D.
(Chester) 15.8.47 and
scrapped.

Grand Rapids
Hull No: PF.31

Launched:
10.9.43

Built by: As above

Sold Sun Sbdg. & D.D.
(Chester) 14.4.47 and
scrapped.

Woonsocket
Hull No: PF.32

Launched:
27.9.43

Built by: As above

Peruvian Navy Teniente
Galvez (1948).

Dearborn
(ex-Toledo)
Hull No: PF.33

Launched:
27.9.43

Built by: As above

Sold 8.4.47
and scrapped.

Long Beach
Hull No: PF.34

Launched:
5.5.43

Built by: Consolidated
Steel (Wilmington)

Soviet Navy EK.2
(1945–49). Japanese
M.S.D.F. Shii (1953–70).

Belfast
Hull No: PF.35

Launched:
20.5.43

Built by: As above

Soviet Navy EK.3
(1945–49); wrecked off
Petropavlovsk 17.11.48.

Glendale
Hull No: PF.36

Launched:
28.5.43

Built by: Consolidated
Steel (Los Angeles)

Soviet Navy EK.4
(1945–49), R.Th.N.
Tachin (1951).

San Pedro
Hull No: PF.37

Launched:
11.6.43

Built by: As above

Soviet Navy EK.5
(1945–49), Japanese
M.S.D.F. Kaya (1953).

Coronado
Hull No: PF.38

Launched:
17.6.43

Built by: Consolidated
(Los Angeles)

Soviet Navy EK.6
(1945–49), Japanese
M.S.D.F. Sugi (1953).

Ogden
Hull No: PF.39

Launched:
23.6.43

Built by: As above

Soviet Navy EK.7
(1945–49), Japanese
M.S.D.F. Kusu (1953).

El Paso
Hull No: PF.41

Launched:
16.7.43

Built by: Consolidated
Steel (Wilmington)

Cuban Navy Jose Marti
(1947).

Eugene
Hull No: PF.40

Launched:
6.7.43

Built by: As above

Sold 14.10.47
and scrapped.

Van Buren
Hull No: PF.42

Launched:
27.7.43

Built by: As above

Sold 1947
and scrapped.

Orange
Hull No: PF.43

Launched:
6.8.43

Built by: As above

Sold Alaska Junk Co.
(Seattle, 17.9.47
and scrapped.

Corpus Christie
Hull No: PF.44

Launched:
17.8.43

Built by: As above

Sold 3.10.47
and scrapped.

Below: The HURON (10 Mar 1945): note HF/DF coil on top of the stump mainmast, and TBS aerials on the yardarms. Unlike British frigates the all-welded hull was not pierced for portholes, and all quarters were mechanically ventilated. A deckhouse and an extended fo'c'sle deck has replaced the 3in and three 20mm A.A. guns aft in the WOONSOCKET (18 Sep 1944) (bottom) to suit her employment as a weather ship. PHOTOGRAPHS: U.S. NAVY

Hutchinson
Hull No: PF.45

Launched:
27.8.43

Built by: Consolidated
Steel (Los Angeles)

Mexican Navy *California*
(1947); sold 6.64 and
scrapped.

Bisbee
Hull No: PF.46

Launched:
7.9.43

Built by: As above

Soviet Navy *EK.18*
(1945–49), Colombian
Navy *Capitan Tono* (1952).

Gallup
Hull No: PF.47

Launched:
17.9.43

Built by: Consolidated
Steel (Los Angeles)

Soviet Navy *EK.19*
(1945–49), R.Th.N.
Prasae (1951).

Rockford
Hull No: PF.48

Launched:
27.9.43

Built by: As above

Soviet Navy *EK.20*
(1945–49), South Korean
Navy *Apnok* (1950–52);
expended as target
1953.

Muskogee
Hull No: PF.49

Launched:
18.10.43

Built by: Consolidated
Steel (Wilmington)

Soviet Navy *EK.21*
(1945–49), South Navy
Dunman (1950).

Carson City
Hull No: PF.50

Launched:
13.11.43

Built by: As above

Soviet Navy *EK.22*
(1945–49), Japanese
M.S.D.F. *Sakura* (1953),
hulked (1966).

Burlington
Hull No: PF.51

Launched:
7.12.43

Built by: As above

Soviet Navy *EK.23*
(1945–49), Colombian
Navy *Almirante Brion*
(1953).

Allenstown
Hull No:

Launched:
3.7.43

Built by: Froemming
(Millwaukee)

Soviet Navy *EK.8*
(1945–49), Japanese
M.S.D.F. *Ume* (1953),
hulked (1965).

Machias(ii)
Hull No: PF.53

22.8.43

Built by: As above

Soviet Navy *EK.9*
(1945–49), Japanese Navy
Nara (1953); hulked
(YTE.3—1966).

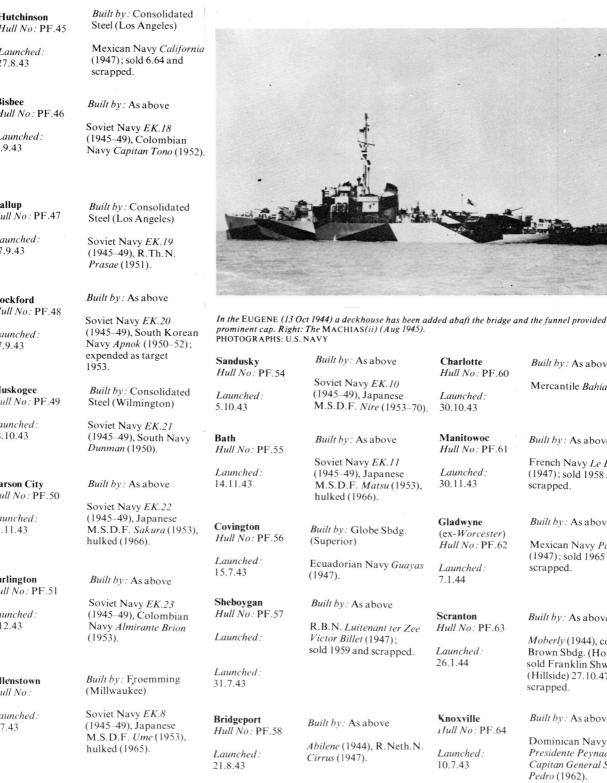

In the EUGENE *(13 Oct 1944) a deckhouse has been added abaft the bridge and the funnel provided with a prominent cap. Right: The* MACHIAS*(ii) (Aug 1945).*
PHOTOGRAPHS: U.S. NAVY

Sandusky
Hull No: PF.54

Launched:
5.10.43

Built by: As above

Soviet Navy *EK.10*
(1945–49), Japanese
M.S.D.F. *Nire* (1953–70).

Bath
Hull No: PF.55

Launched:
14.11.43

Built by: As above

Soviet Navy *EK.11*
(1945–49), Japanese
M.S.D.F. *Matsu* (1953),
hulked (1966).

Covington
Hull No: PF.56

Launched:
15.7.43

Built by: Globe Sbdg.
(Superior)

Ecuadorian Navy *Guayas*
(1947).

Sheboygan
Hull No: PF.57

Launched:

Launched:
31.7.43

Built by: As above

R.B.N. *Luitenant ter Zee
Victor Billet* (1947);
sold 1959 and scrapped.

Bridgeport
Hull No: PF.58

Launched:
21.8.43

Built by: As above

Abilene (1944), R.Neth.N.
Cirrus (1947).

Beaufort
Hull No: PF.59

Launched:
9.10.43

Built by: As above

Sold 11.4.47
and scrapped.

Charlotte
Hull No: PF.60

Launched:
30.10.43

Built by: As above

Mercantile *Bahia* (1950).

Manitowoc
Hull No: PF.61

Launched:
30.11.43

Built by: As above

French Navy *Le Brix*
(1947); sold 1958 and
scrapped.

Gladwyne
(ex-*Worcester*)
Hull No: PF.62

Launched:
7.1.44

Built by: As above

Mexican Navy *Papaloapan*
(1947); sold 1965 and
scrapped.

Scranton
Hull No: PF.63

Launched:
26.1.44

Built by: As above

Moberly (1944), completed
Brown Sbdg. (Houston);
sold Franklin Shwg.
(Hillside) 27.10.47 and
scrapped.

Knoxville
Hull No: PF.64

Launched:
10.7.43

Built by: As above

Dominican Navy
Presidente Peynado (1947),
*Capitan General Santana
Pedro* (1962).

Uniontown
(ex- *Chattanooga*)
Hull No: PF.65

Launched:
7.8.43

Built by: Leatham D.
Smith (Sturgeon Bay)

Argentinian Navy *Sarandi*
(1946); scrapped 1968.

Reading
Hull No: PF.66

Launched:
28.8.43

Built by: As above

Argentinian Navy *Heriona*
(1946); scrapped 1966.

Peoria
Hull No: PF.67

Launched:
2.10.43

Built by: As above

Cuban Navy *Antonio
Maceo* (1947).

Brunswick
Hull No: PF.68

Launched:
6.11.43

Built by: As above

Sold 9.4.47
and scrapped.

Davenport
Hull No: PF.69

Launched:
8.12.43

Built by: As above

Sold 6.6.46
and scrapped.

Evansville
Hull No: PF.70

Launched:
27.11.43

Built by: As above

Soviet Navy *EK.28*
(1945–49), Japanese
M.S.D.F. *Keyaki* (1953).

New Bedford
Hull No: PF.71

Launched
29.12.43

Built by: As above

Sold 11.47 and
scrapped.

Machias(i)
Hull No: PF.72

Launched:
14.7.43

Built by: Walsh-Kaiser
(Providence)

R.N. *Hallowel* (1943),
Anguilla (1943); sold
Pro-Industry Products
(New York) 8.5.47, resold
Soc. de Navigation
Levante (Panama) and
scrapped.

Unnamed
Hull No: PF.73

Built by: Walsh-Kaiser
(Providence)

R.N. *Hammond* (1943),
Antigua (1943);
sold 1947 and scrapped.

Unnamed
Hull No: PF.74

Launched

Built by: As above

R.N. *Hargood* (1943),
Ascension (1943); sold
Hudson Valley Shwg.
(Newburg) 16.10.47 and
scrapped.

Unnamed
Hull No: PF.75

Launched:
17.8.43

Built by: As above

R.N. *Hotham* (1943),
Bahamas (1943); sold John
J. Duane (Quincy) 16.12.47
and scrapped.

Unnamed
Hull No: PF.76

Launched:
27.8.43

Built by: As above

R.N. *Halsted* (1943),
Barbados (1943); sold Sun
Sbdg. & D.D. (Chester)
30.10.47 and scrapped.

Unnamed
Hull No: PF.77

Launched:
6.9.43

Built by: As above

R.N. *Hannam* (1943),
Caicos (1943), Argentinian
Navy *Trinidad* (1947),
Comodoro Augusto Lasere
(1963); scrapped 1970.

Unnamed
Hull No: PF.78

Launched:
6.9.43

Built by: As above

R.N. *Harland* (1943),
Cayman (1943); sold
United Dock (New York)
1.7.47 and scrapped.

Unnamed
Hull No: PF.79

Launched:
14.9.43

Built by: As above

R.N. *Harman* (1943),
Dominica (1943); sold Sun
Sbdg. & D.D. (Chester)
27.3.47 and scrapped.

Unnamed
Hull No: PF.80

Launched:
21.9.43

Built by: As above

R.N. *Harvey* (1943), *Gold
Coast* (1943), *Labuan*
(1943); sold Heggie Iron
& Metal (Dorchester)
9.7.47 and scrapped.

Unnamed
Hull No: PF.81

Launched:
27.9.43

Built by: As above

R.N. *Holmes* (1943), *Hong
Kong* (1943), *Tobago*
(1943); mercantile (name
unchanged—1950);
conversion abandoned
1956 and scrapped Egypt.

Unnamed
Hull No: PF.82

Launched:
27.9.43

Built by: Walsh-Kaiser
(Providence)

R.N. *Hornby* (1943),
Montserrat (1943); sold
John J. Duane (Quincy
30.11.47 and scrapped.

Unnamed
Hull No: PF.83

Launched:
7.9.43

Built by: As above

R.N. *Hoste* (1943),
Nyasaland (1943); sold
Sun Sbdg. & D.D.
(Chester) 15.11.47 and
scrapped.

Unnamed
Hull No: PF.84

Launched:
10.10.43

Built by: As above

R.N. *Howett* (1943),
Papua (1943), mercantile
(name unchanged—1950);
conversion abandoned
1956 and scrapped Egypt.

Unnamed *Hull No:* PF.85 *Launched:* 15.10.43	*Built by:* As above R.N. *Pilford* (1943), *Pitcairn* (1943); sold John J. Duane (Quincy) 8.11.47 and scrapped.	**Unnamed** *Hull No:* PF.89 *Launched:* 5.11.43	*Built by:* As above R.N. *Phillimore* (1943), *Sierra Leone* (1943), *Perim* (1943); sold 1947 and scrapped.
Unnamed *Hull No:* PF.86 *Launched:* 20.10.43	*Built by:* As above R.N. *Pasley* (1943), *St. Helena* (1943); sold 1947 and scrapped.	**Unnamed** *Hull No:* PF.90 *Launched:* 11.11.43	*Built by:* As above R.N. *Popham* (1943), *Somaliland* (1943); sold 1947 and scrapped.
Unnamed *Hull No:* PF.87 *Launched:* 25.10.43	*Built by:* As above R.N. *Patton* (1943), *Sarawak* (1943); sold 1947 and scrapped.	**Unnamed** *Hull No:* PF.91 *Launched:* 16.11.43	*Built by:* Walsh-Kaiser (Providence) R.N. *Peyton* (1943), *Tortola* (1943); sold 1947 and scrapped.
Unnamed *Hull No:* PF.88 *Launched:* 30.10.43	*Built by:* As above R.N. *Peard* (1943), *Seychelles* (1943); sold 1947 and scrapped.	**Unamed** *Hull No:* PF.92 *Launched:* 21.11.43	*Built by:* As above R.N. *Prowse* (1943), *Zanzibar* (1943); sold 1947 and scrapped.

Lorain(ii) (ex-*Roanoke*) *Hull No:* PF.93 *Launched:* 18.3.44	*Built by:* American Sbdg. (Lorain) French Navy *Laplace* (1947); mined (place unknown) 16.9.50.
Milledgeville(ii) (ex-*Sitka*) *Hull No:* PF.94 *Launched:* 5.4.44	*Built by:* As above Sold Southern Scrap Materials, arrived New Orleans 25.3.48 and scrapped.
Stamford *Hull No:* PF.95	*Built by:* As above Cancelled 31.12.43.
Macon *Hull No:* PF.96	*Built by:* As above Cancelled 31.12.43.
Lorain(i) (ex-*Vallejo*) *Hull No:* PF.97	*Built by:* As above Cancelled 11.1.44.
Milledgeville(i) *Hull No:* PF.98	*Built by:* As above Cancelled 31.12.43 and scrapped on slip.
Orlando *Hull No:* PF.99 *Launched:* 1.12.43	*Built by:* American Sbdg. (Cleveland) Sold Zidell Ship Dismantling 10.11.47 and scrapped Seattle.
Racine *Hull No:* PF.100 *Launched:* 15.3.44	*Built by:* American Sbdg. (Cleveland) Sold 12.47 and scrapped.
Greenboro *Hull No:* PF.101 *Launched:* 9.2.44	*Built by:* As above Sold Southern Scrap Materials (New Orleans) 22.4.48 and scrapped.
Forsyth *Hull No:* 102 *Launched:* 20.5.44	*Built by:* As above R.Neth.N. *Cumulus* (1947).

Below: The BEAUFORT *(6 Sep 1944) was another unit employed on weather observation and plane guard duties in the North Atlantic. Bottom: The* PEORIA *(June 1945) with modified rig: the HF/DF coil has been moved to forward of the bridge, the SW.RDF is carried higher and abaft the AW set at the masthead, and a light tripod mainmast has been stepped to spread the W/T aerials.*   PHOTOGRAPHS: U.S. NAVY

Armed Yachts

In addition to the larger yachts a number of smaller yachts were also acquired for inshore and harbour patrol work by the United States Navy in 1941–42. Most were classed as coastal armed yachts (PYc), but a few of the faster units were initially rated patrol craft (PC) until 1943 when they were re-classed as PYc. They were soon replaced by naval-designed steel patrol craft built under the war programmes, and with few exceptions most of the coastal yachts were relegated to training and subsidiary harbour duties by 1943–44.

Not all the craft requisitioned were finally placed in service as coastal yachts. The *Sard*, *Iolite(i)*, and *Brave* were re-classed as unnamed harbour patrol craft (YP); the *Tourist* and *Palace* as unnamed harbour auxiliaries (YAG); while the *Agate* and *Captor* were ex-trawlers originally acquired for conversion to minesweepers (AM); and the *Vagrant* was uprated from the unnamed harbour craft *YP.258*. In 1943 the *Perseverance* was transferred from the United States Coast Guard, and the *Black Douglas* was re-classed from a miscellaneous auxiliary (IX.55).

A very varied armament was shipped by coastal yachts: some mounted one/two 3in guns and others only had machine guns, but all were fitted with sonar and depth charges. Nearly all were of steel construction and diesel-engined, but a few of the smaller craft had wood hulls and some of the older units had steam reciprocating machinery.

Armed yachts ARGUS *(below – 1 Aug 1941) and* CARNELIAN *(bottom – 1 Oct 1942).*

Ex-yacht: **ISABEL**
710 tons: 230(pp) $245\frac{3}{4}$(oa) $\times 27\frac{3}{4} \times 8\frac{1}{2}$ feet: two Norman boilers, two shafts, Parsons turbines S.H.P. 8,400 = 26 knots. O.F. 216 tons: two 3-inch A.A. (2 × 1) guns: complement 99.

Ex-yacht: **SYLPH**
597 tons *gross:* 152(pp) 205(oa) $\times 33\frac{3}{4} \times 17\frac{1}{2}$d/16 feet: one shaft, 6-cyl. Winton diesel engine (bore 17″ × 26″ stroke) B.H.P. 1,000, speed not known, oil fuel: one 3-inch gun: complement not known.

Ex-yacht: **SIREN**
720 tons: $168\frac{3}{4}$(pp) $205\frac{3}{4}$(oa) $\times 28\frac{1}{4} \times 14\frac{1}{4}$d/$10\frac{1}{4}$ feet: two shafts, 6-cyl. Winton diesel engines (bore 14″ × 16″ stroke) B.H.P. 1,000 = 12 knots, oil fuel: two 3-inch/50cal (2 × 1), two 3-inch A.A. (2 × 1) guns: complement 89.

Ex-yacht: **ARGUS**
859 tons: 178(pp) 218(oa) $\times 30 \times 17\frac{1}{4}$/12 feet: two shafts, 6-cyl. Krupp diesel engines (bore 430mm × 550mm stroke) B.H.P. 1,500 = $13\frac{1}{2}$ knots, oil fuel: one 3-inch gun: complement 59.

Ex-yacht: **CORAL**
790 tons: $191\frac{1}{4}$(pp) $214\frac{1}{2}$(oa) $\times 26\frac{1}{2} \times$ . .d/13 feet: two shafts, 4-cyl. Doxford diesel engines (bore 13″ × 39″ stroke) B.H.P. 1500 = $14\frac{1}{2}$ knots, oil fuel: two 3-inch (2 × 1) guns: complement not known.

Isabel (ex-yacht) *Hull No:* PY.10 *Launched:* 28.12.17	*Built by:* Bath I.W. Sold 25.3.46 and scrapped.
Sylph ex-yacht *Intrepid*) *Hull No:* PY.12 *Launched:* 5.30	*Built by:* G. Lawley (Neponset) Yacht *Sylph* (1947); sold 1960 and scrapped.
Siren (ex-yacht *Lotosland*) *Hull No:* PY.13 *Launched:* 1929	*Built by:* Pusey & Jones (Wilmington) Disposal unknown.
Argus (ex-yacht *Haido*) *Hull No:* PY.14 *Launched:* 1929	*Built by:* Germaniawerft (Kiel) Transferred Maritime Commission 30.10.46 for disposal.
Coral (ex-yacht *Yankee Clipper*, ex-*Sialia*) *Hull No:* PY.15 *Launched:* 1913	*Built by:* Pusey & Jones (Wilmington) Expended as target 1944.

Of the large numbers of yachts requisitioned for naval service those over 1,000 tons gross were classed as gunboats, while those between 500–1,000 tons gross were classed as sea-going armed yachts (PY), and those under 500 tons gross as coastal armed yachts (PYc).

With the exception of the *Isabel* the first ten sea-going armed yachts (PY.12–21) were acquired pre-war during 1940–41, and the remainder in 1941–42 after the outbreak of hostilities. The *Isabel* was requisitioned by the United States Navy while building in 1917, and owing to her high speed—26 knots—was first classed as a destroyer (SP.521). She was retained in naval service after the war, and was mainly employed as a gunboat although classed as an armed yacht (PY). The original intention was to convert the *Siren* into a coastal minelayer (CMc.1) but it was decided not to proceed with this proposal, the *Turquoise* was first classed as the patrol craft *PC.459*, while the *Hydrographer* was not finally placed in service as an armed yacht but remained on surveying duties.

Ex-yacht: **ZIRCON**
958 tons *gross*: 196½(pp) 234¾(oa) × 34¼ × 16¾d/12 feet: two shafts, 8-cyl. Winton diesel engines (bore 16½″ × 26″ stroke) (B.H.P. not known) 14 knots, oil fuel: two 3-inch A.A. (2 × 1) guns: complement not known.

Ex-yacht: **JADE**
582 tons: 162¾(wl) 171(oa) × 27½ × 16½d/13 feet: two shafts, 6-cyl. Cooper-Bessemer diesel engines (bore 16″ = 22″ stroke) B.H.P. 1,600 = 14 knots, oil fuel: four ·3-inch A.A. (4 × 1) guns: complement 26.

Ex-yacht: **TURQUOISE**
565 tons: 163½(wl) 172(oa) × 26 × 14½d/11 feet: two shafts, 6-cyl. Winton diesel engines (bore 13″ × 18″ stroke) B.H.P. 700 = 10 knots, oil fuel: one 3-inch, two 20mm A.A. (2 × 1) guns: complement not known.

Ex-yachts: **CARNELIAN, TOURMALINE-RUBY**
502 tons *gross*: 154(pp) 191(oa) × 26½ × 14½d/10 feet: two shafts, 8-cyl. Cooper-Bessemer diesel engines (bore 11″ × 14″ stroke) B.H.P. 850 = 12 knots, oil fuel: two 3-inch A.A. (2 × 1) guns: complement 59.

Ex-yacht: **AZURLITE**
951 tons: 182(pp) 222(oa) × 33¾ × 16d/12 feet: two shafts, 6-cyl. Krupp diesel engines (bore 400mm × 670mm stroke) (B.H.P. not known) 12 knots, oil fuel: two 3-inch (2 × 1) guns: complement 67.

Ex-yacht: **BERYL**
1029 tons: 196½(pp) 234¾(oa) × 34¼ × 16¾d/12 feet: two shafts, 8-cyl. Winton diesel engines (bore 16½″ × 26″ stroke) (B.H.P. not known) 14 knots, oil fuel: two 3-inch (2 × 1) guns: complement 66.

The yacht ZIRCON *(30 Apr 1944) was armed with two 3in A.A. (2 × 1) and two 20mm A.A. (2 × 1) guns, and was fitted with SW.RDF at the masthead.* PHOTOGRAPH: U.S. NAVY

Zircon (ex-yacht *Nakhoda*) Hull No: PY.16	*Built by:* As above Yacht *New York* (1951).
Launched: 1930	
Jade (ex-yacht *Doctor Brinkley*, ex-*Caroline*, ex-*Athero II*) Hull No: PY.17	*Built by:* G. Lawley (Neponset) Ecuadorian Navy (name unchanged—1943–44); yacht *Santa Maria* (1946).
Launched: ...9.26	
Turquoise (ex-*PC.459*, ex-yacht *Entropy*, ex-*Kallisto*, ex-*Walucia III*, ex-*Miramichi*, ex-*Ohio*) Hull No: PY.18	*Built by:* Newport News Ecuadorian Navy *Neuve de Octubre* (1944), *Esmeralda* (1951); lost unknown cause Guayaquil 7.9.53.
Launched: 1922	
Carnelian (ex-yacht *Seventeen*, ex-*Trudione*) Hull No: PY.19	*Built by:* Bath I.W. Yacht *William Johnson* (post-war)
Launched: 1930	
Tourmaline (ex-yacht *Sylvia*) Hull No: PY.20	*Built by:* As above Yacht *Sylvia* (1946), *Adelphic* (1946), *Kyknos* (1948).
Launched: 1930	
Ruby (ex-yacht *Placida*) Hull No: PY.21	*Built by:* As above Yacht *Placida* (1947); lost cause and place unknown 2.12.56.
Launched: 1930	
Azurlite (ex-yacht *Vagabond*) Hull No: PY.22	*Built by:* Germanaiwerft (Kiel) Yacht *Azurlite* (1947), *Pacific Reefer* (1969).
Launched: 11.28	
Beryl (ex-yacht *Rene*) Hull No: PY.23	*Built by:* Pusey & Jones (Wilmington) Yacht *Baltimore* (1947).
Launched: 1.30	

Ex-yacht: **ALMANDITE**
256 tons: 165¼(pp) 196½(oa) × 27 × 14d/11½ feet: two shafts, 6-cyl. Krupp diesel engines (bore 300mm × 550mm stroke) (B.H.P. not known) 12 knots, oil fuel: one 3-inch gun: complement 75.

Ex-yacht: **CRYSTAL**
954 tons *gross*: 196½(pp) 234¾(oa) × 34¼ × 16¾d/12 feet: two shafts, 8-cyl. Winton diesel engines (bore 16½″ × 26″ stroke) (B.H.P. not known) 18 knots, oil fuel: two 3-inch (2 × 1) guns: complement not known.

Ex-yacht: **CYTHERA(i)**
1,000 tons: 179½(pp) 214¾(oa) × 27½ × 16¾d/12 feet: two SE cylindrical boilers (180lb/in²), one shaft, reciprocating (VTE—cyl. 17″:27″:31″(2) × 27″ stroke) (I.H.P. not known) 12 knots, oil fuel: three 3-inch (3 × 1) guns: complement 113.

Ex-yacht: **GIRASOL**
700 tons: 170(oa) × 27 × 11 feet: two shafts. Krupp diesel engines (B.H.P. not known) 12 knots, oil fuel: one 3-inch, two 20mm A.A. (2 × 1) guns: complement 55.

Ex-yacht: **MARCASITE**
1,130 tons: 181½(pp) 225¼(oa) × 2½ × 21¼d/14½ feet: two shafts, 6-cyl. Cooper-Bessemer diesel engines (bore 16″ × 20″ stroke) (B.H.P. not known) 12 knots, oil fuel: two 3-inch A.A. (2 × 1) guns: complement 120.

Ex-yacht: **MIZPAH**
607 tons: 174(pp) 185(oa) × 27¼ × 12¾d/10 feet: two shafts, 6-cyl. Winton diesel engines (bore 16½″ × 22″ stroke) (B.H.P. not known) 14 knots, oil fuel: two 3-inch (2 × 1), three ·5-inch A.A. (3 × 1) guns: complement 62.

Ex-yacht: **HYDROGRAPHER**
Not placed in service as armed yacht.

Ex-yacht: **CYTHERA(ii)**
800 tons: 205½(oa) × 30 × 10¾ feet: two shafts, Krupp diesel engines (B.H.P. not known) 15 knots, oil fuel: one 3-inch gun: complement 74.

Ex-yacht: **SOUTHERN SEAS**
819 tons gross: 200(pp) 230(oa) × 30¼ × 19d/15 feet: two shafts, 6-cyl. B & W diesel engines (bore 400mm × 480mm stroke) (B.H.P. and speed not known), oil fuel: guns and complement not known.

Ex-yacht: **EMERALD**
75 tons: 99¾(oa) × 16 feet: two shafts, diesel engines (B.H.P. not known) 14 knots, oil fuel: guns not known: complement 32.

Ex-yacht: **SAPPHIRE**
466 tons gross: 155¼(pp) 165¼(oa) × 25¼ × 14¼d/10 feet: two shafts, 8-cyl. Cooper-Bessemer diesel engines (bore 11″ × 14″ stroke) (B.H.P. and speed not known), oil fuel: one 3-inch/23cal gun: complement not known.

Almandite (ex-yacht *Happy Days*) Hull No: PY.24
Launched: 1927
Built by: Germaniawerft (Kiel)
Transferred War Shpg. Admin. 5.12.46 for disposal.

Crystal (ex-yacht *Vida*, ex-*Cambriona*) Hull No: PY.25
Launched: 5.30
Built by: Pusey & Jones (Wilmington)
Transferred Maritime Commission 2.4.47 for disposal.

Cythera(i) (ex-yacht *Cythera*, ex-*Agawa*) Hull No: PY.26
Launched: 1.07
Built by: Ramage & Ferguson (Leith)
Torpedoed German submarine *U.402* off North Carolina coast 2.5.42.

Girasol (ex-yacht *Firenze*) Hull No: PY.27
Launched: 1926
Built by: Germaniawerft (Kiel)
Yacht *South Seas* (1947).

Marcasite (ex-yacht *Ramfis*, ex-*Camargo*) Hull No: PY.28
Launched: 8.28
Built by: G. Lawley (Neponset)
Yacht *Commando* (1946) *Westminster* (1947), *Star of Malta* (1952).

Mizpah (ex-yacht *Mizpah*, ex-*Allegro*, ex-*Savarona*) Hull No: PY.29
Launched: 1926
Built by: Newport News
Transferred War Shpg. Admin. 25.9.46 for disposal.

Hydrographer (ex-USC & GS) Hull No: PY.30
Launched: 1930
Built by: Spear Engine (Norfolk)
AGS.2 (142); retroceded U.S.C. & G.S. (1946).

Cythera(ii) (ex-yacht *Abril*) Hull No: PY.31
Launched: 1931
Built by: Germaniawerft (Kiel)
Yacht *Abril* (1945), Israeli Navy *Ben Hecht* (19. .), yacht *Santa Maria del Mare* (1950).

Southern Seas (ex-yacht *Lyndonia*) Hull No: PY.32
Launched: 1920
Built by: Consolidated Sbdg. (Morris Heights)
Foundered stress of weather off Okinawa 8.10.45.

Machinery contracts: Sylph, Siren, Zircon, Jade, Turquoise, Beryl, Crystal, and *Mizpah* Mizpah engined by Winton; *Argus, Azurlite, Almandite, Girasol,* and *Cythera(ii)* by Fried. Krupp; *Coral* by Sun Sbdg.; *Carnelian, Tourmaline, Ruby,* and *Marcasite* by Cooper Bessemer; *Southern Seas* by Burmeister & Wain: and others by builders.

Emerald (ex-yacht *Savitor*) Hull No: PYc.1
Completed: 1922
Built by: Consolidated Sbdg. (Morris Heights)
Transferred Maritime Commission 13.11.45 for disposal.

Sapphire (ex-yacht *Buccaneer*, ex-*Margo*, ex-*Comco*). Hull No: PYc.2
Completed: 1929
Built by: G. Lawley (Neponset)
Sold 1945.

Mast details of the armed yacht TOURMALINE *(23 Nov 1944) have been obliterated by the war-time censor.*
PHOTOGRAPH: U.S. NAVY

Ex-yacht : **AMETHYST**
525 tons: $127\frac{1}{4}$(pp) $146\frac{3}{4}$(oa) $\times 23\frac{1}{2} \times 13d/11$ feet: two shafts, 6-cyl. Winton diesel engines (bore $14'' \times 16''$ stroke) (B.H.P. not known) $14\frac{1}{2}$ knots, oil fuel: one 3-inch gun: complement 46.

Ex-yacht : **AGATE**
See under auxiliary minesweeper *Goldcrest(i)* for details.

Ex-yacht : **ONYX**
190 tons *gross:* $110\frac{1}{4}$(pp) $118\frac{1}{2}$(oa) $\times 21\frac{1}{2} \times 10\frac{1}{2}d/$ 8 feet: two shafts, 6-cyl. Winton diesel engines (bore $9\frac{1}{2}'' \times 14''$ stroke) (B.H.P. not known) 12 knots, oil fuel: one 3-inch, six ·3-inch (6×1) guns: complement not known.

Ex-yacht : **AMBER**
260 tons: 114(pp) 120(oa) $\times 21\frac{1}{2} \times 13\frac{1}{2}d/8\frac{3}{4}$ feet: two shafts, 6-cyl. Atlas diesel engines (bore $11\frac{1}{2}'' \times 15''$ stroke) (B.H.P. not known) 11 knots, oil fuel: one 3-inch gun: complement not known.

Ex-yacht : **AQUAMARINE**
215 tons: 124(oa) $\times 20\frac{1}{2} \times 15d$: two shafts, Union diesel engines B.H.P. $1,200 = 12$ knots, oil fuel: two 3-inch (2×1) guns: complement 36.

Ex-yacht : **OPAL**
590 tons: 150(pp) $185\frac{1}{2}$(oa) $\times 27 \times 15\frac{1}{2}d/10$ feet: two shafts, 6-cyl Krupp diesel engines (bore 300mm $\times$ 550mm bore) B.H.P. $800 = 13$ knots, oil fuel: two 3-inch (2×1), four ·5-inch (4×1) guns: complement 50.

Ex-yacht : **ANDRADITE**
322 tons: $132\frac{1}{4}$(pp) $140\frac{1}{4}$(oa) $\times 23\frac{1}{2} \times 12d/8\frac{3}{4}$ feet: two shafts, 6-cyl. Cooper-Bessemer diesel engines (bore $10\frac{1}{2}'' \times 14''$ stroke) (B.H.P. not known) $11\frac{1}{2}$ knots, oil fuel: one 3-inch gun: complement 56.

Ex-yacht : **SARDONYX**
475 tons *gross:* 150(pp) $185\frac{1}{2}$(oa) $\times 27 \times 14d/$ $10\frac{1}{2}$ feet: two shafts, 4-cyl. Krupp diesel engines (bore 300mm $\times$ 550mm stroke) B.H.P. $550 = 11$ knots, oil fuel: guns and complement not known.

Ex-yacht : **JASPER**
395 tons: 125(pp) 135(oa) $\times 22\frac{3}{4} \times 16\frac{1}{2}d/13\frac{1}{2}$ feet: two shafts, diesel engines B.H.P. $800 =$ 12 knots, oil fuel: two 3-inch (2×1) guns: complement not known.

Ex-yacht : **TRUANT**
221 tons *gross:* $111\frac{3}{4}$(pp) $121\frac{1}{4}$(oa) $\times 21 \times 9\frac{1}{2}d/$ $4\frac{1}{4}$ feet: two shafts, 8-cyl. Winton diesel engines (bore $8'' \times 10''$ stroke) (B.H.P. and speed not known), oil fuel: guns and complement not known.

Ex-yacht : **GARNET**
490 tons: 147(pp) $156\frac{3}{4}$(oa) $\times 25\frac{1}{2} \times 12\frac{1}{4}d/9\frac{1}{2}$ feet: two shafts, 6-cyl. Krupp diesel engines (bore 350mm $\times$ 350mm stroke) (B.H.P. not known) 12 knots, oil fuel: one 3-inch, four ·5-inch (4×1), two ·3-inch (2×1) guns: complement 50.

Ex-yacht : **CHALCEDONY**
500 tons: 192(pp) 195(oa) $\times 30 \times 16\frac{1}{2}d/11\frac{3}{4}$ feet: two shafts, 6-cyl. Winton diesel engines (bore $17'' \times 26''$ stroke) (B.H.P. not known) $= 14$ knots, oil fuel: one 3-inch gun: complement not known.

Amethyst
(ex-yacht *Samona II*)
Hull No: PYc.3

Completed:
1931

Built by: Craig. Sbdg. (Long Beach)

Transferred Maritime Commission 11.9.46 for disposal.

Agate
(ex-*Goldcrest* ex-yacht *Stella Polaris* ex-*Armina*)
Hull No: PYc.4

Launched:
1930

Built by: Mathis Yacht (Camden)

Transferred Maritime Commission 3.7.45 for disposal.

Onyx
(ex-yacht *Pegasus*, ex-*Rene*, ex-*Janey III*)
Hull No: PYc.5

Launched:
1924

Built by: Consolidated Sbdg. (Morris Heights)

Stricken 8.2.45 and

Amber
(ex-yacht *Polaris*, ex-*Infanta*)
Hull No. PYc.6

Launched:
1930

Built by: Lake Union D.D. (Seattle)

Transferred Maritime Commission 13.6.45 for disposal.

Aquamarine
(ex-yacht *Seawolf*, ex-*Clader*, ex-*Vasanta*)
Hull No: PYc.7

Launched:
1926

Built by: Pusey & Jones (Wilmington)

Transferred Maritime Commission 31.1.47 for disposal.

Opal
(ex-yacht *Coronet*)
Hull No: PYc.8

Launched:
1928

Built by: Germaniawerft (Kiel)

Ecuadorian Navy *Diez de Agosto* (1943), *Manabi* (1951); scrapped 1960.

Moonstone
(ex-yacht *Lone Star*, ex-*Mona*, ex-*Nancy Baker*)
Hull No: PYc.9

Launched:
1929

Built by: Germaniawerft (Kiel)

Collision destroyer *Greer* off Delaware Capes 16/10/43.

Topaz
(ex-yacht *Doromar*)
Hull No: PYc.10

Launched:
3.31

Built by: Luders Marine (Stamford)

Retroceded 1944.

Andradite
(ex-yacht *Caronia*, ex-*Comeco*)
Hull No: PYc.11

Launched:
1927

Built by: Defoe Boat & Motor (Bay City)

U.S.C. & G.S. (1946).

Sardonyx
(ex-yacht *Queen Anne*)
Hull No: PYc.12

Launched:
1928

Built by: Germaniawerft (Kiel)

Sold 1945.

The yacht RUBY *(8 Nov 1943) armed with two 3in A.A. (2×1) and four A.A. (4×1) machine guns, and fitted with SW.RDF at the masthead.* PHOTOGRAPH: U.S. NAVY

Ex-yacht: PYROPE
490 tons: 149(pp) 156¼(oa) × 24¾ × 13¼d/9½ feet: two shafts, 6-cyl. Krupp diesel engines (bore 350mm × 350mm stroke) (B.H.P. not known) 12½ knots, oil fuel: one 3-inch, one 40mm A.A. guns: complement not known.

Ex-yacht: PERIDOT
300 tons: 133½(pp) 144½(oa) × 23 × 12½/8 feet: two shafts, diesel engines (B.H.P. not known) 13 knots, oil fuel: one 3-inch, six ·5-inch (6 × 1) guns: complement 48.

Ex-yacht: RHODOLITE
485 tons *gross:* 150(pp) 154¾(oa) × 26 × 15d/8½ feet: two shafts, 8-cyl. Cooper-Bessemer diesel engines (bore 11″ × 14″ stroke) (B.H.P. and speed not known), oil fuel: guns and complement not known.

Ex-yacht: JET
386 tons *gross:* 158½(pp) 160(oa) × 24½ × 12½d/8½ feet: two shafts, 6-cyl. Winton diesel engines (bore 14″ × 16″ stroke) (B.H.P. not known) = 15 knots, oil fuel: one 3-inch gun: complement not known.

Ex-yacht: ALABASTER
306 tons: 146¾(pp) 148(oa) × 23 × 12½d/8 feet: two shafts, 6-cyl. Winton diesel engines (bore 11″ × 15″ stroke) (B.H.P. not known) 14½ knots, oil fuel: one 40mm A.A. gun: complement 48.

Ex-yacht: MOONSTONE
645 tons: 161¾(pp) 171¾(oa) × 26¾ × 13¼d/10½ feet: two shafts, 6-cyl. Krupp diesel engines (bore 300mm × 550mm stroke) B.H.P. 800 = 12 knots, oil fuel: one 3-inch, two ·5-inch (2 × 1) guns: complement 50.

Ex-yacht: TOPAZE
152 tons *gross:* 102¾(pp) 111¾(oa) × 20 × 9d/7 feet: two shafts, 8-cyl. Winton diesel engines (bore 8″ × 10″ stroke) (B.H.P. and speed not known), oil fuel: guns and complement not known.

Jasper
(ex-yacht *Stranger*)
Hull No: PYc.13

Launched:
1938

Truant
(ex-yacht *Truant*)
Hull No: PYc.14

Launched:
1930

Garnet
(ex-yacht *Caritas*)
Hull No: PYc.15

Launched:
1925

Chalcedony
(ex-yacht *Valero III*)
Hull No: PYc.16

Launched:
1931

Pyrope
(ex-yacht *Oceania*, ex-*Oceanus*)
Hull No: PYc.17

Launched:
1923

Built by: Lake Union D.D. (Seattle)

Transferred Maritime Commission 6.48 for disposal.

Built by: Mathis Yacht (Camden)

Retroceded 1943.

Built by: Germaniawerft (Kiel)

Sold I.W. Lambert (Baltimore) 10.6.47.

Built by: Craig. Sbdg. (Long Beach)

Transferred Maritime Commission 17.10.46 for disposal.

Built by: Germaniawerft (Kiel)

Sold Juan Perlo (Los Angeles) 29.1.47.

Peridot
(ex-yacht *Bymar*)
Hull No: PYc.18

Launched:
1938

Rhodolite
Seapine,
ex-*Yankee*,
ex-*Seapine*)
Hull PYc.19

Launched:
5.31

Jet
(ex-yacht *Thalia*)
Hull No: PYc.20

Launched:
1930

Alabaster
(ex-yacht *Ronaele*,
ex-*Ranley*,
ex-*Rellimpa*,
ex-*Alamo*)
Hull No: PYc.21

Launched:
1932

Built by: Defoe Boat & Motor (Bay City)

Yacht *Bymar* (1947), *Mimosan* (1953), *Halimede* (later).

Built by: Bath I.W.

Sold 1945.

Built by: Defoe Boat & Motor (Bay City)

Transferred Maritime Commission 20.9.47 for disposal.

Built by: Mathis Yacnt (Camden)

Transferred War Shpg. Admin. 8.4.47 for disposal.

Armed yacht GIRASOL *(20 June 1942)*.   PHOTOGRAPH: U.S. NAVY

1

2

3

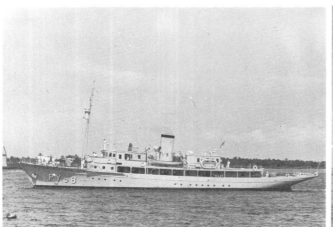

4

5

(1) Armed yacht MARCASITE *(30 Aug 1943).* PHOTOGRAPH: U.S. NAVY

(2) Armed yacht SAPPHIRE *(8 July 1941).* PHOTOGRAPH: U.S. NAVY

(3) The yacht AGATE *(14 Feb 1941) armed with two A.A. (2×1) machine guns on the wheelhouse roof.*
PHOTOGRAPH: U.S. NAVY

(4) The yacht OPAL *(19 July 1941) armed with a 3in/23cal on the fo'c'sle: note large peace-time hull number.*
PHOTOGRAPH: U.S. NAVY

(5) Armed yacht ANDRODITE *(1 Aug 1941).* PHOTOGRAPH: U.S. NAVY

Above: The yacht CYMOPHANE *(5 Sep 1942) armed with a 3in A.A. gun aft and two ·5in A.A. (2×1)
machine guns.* PHOTOGRAPH: U.S. NAVY

Below: The yacht ABILITY *(16 Oct 1942) was armed with a 4in gun aft and three ·5in A.A. (3×1) machine
guns. Additional bow and profile views are shown on pp. 26 & 27.* PHOTOGRAPHS: U.S. NAVY

Ex-yacht: **ABILITY**
241 tons: 125½(pp) 133(oa) × 21½ × 11d/7¾
feet: two shafts, 6-cyl. Cooper-Bessemer diesel
engines (bore 9½″ × 14″ stroke) (B.H.P. not
known) 13 knots, oil fuel: one 4-inch, three
·5-inch A.A. (3 × 1) guns: complement 13.

Ex-yacht: **GALLANT**
310 tons *gross:* 146½(pp) 189(oa) × 23½ ×
12½d/11 feet: one boiler, one shaft,
reciprocating (VTE—cyl. 14″:21″:24″(2) × 18″
stroke) (I.H.P. not known) 13 knots, oil fuel:
one 3-inch, one 20mm A.A., one 5-inch gun:
complement not known.

Ex-yacht: **VAGRANT**
178 tons *gross:* 80(pp) 109(oa) × 24¾ × 16d/15
feet: two shafts, 6-cyl. Speedway petrol
engines (bore 5¾″ × 7″ stroke) (B.H.P. and
speed not known), gasoline fuel: guns and
complement not known.

Ex-yacht: **LASH**
339 tons: 153¼(pp) 187¾(oa) × 24 × 12½d/9¾
feet: two w.t. boilers, one shaft, reciprocating
(VTE—cyl. 13½″: 21″: 24″ × 24″ stroke) (I.H.P.
not known) 14 knots, oil fuel: two 3-inch
(2 × 1) guns: complement not known.

Ex-yacht: **TOURIST**
Not placed in service as armed yacht.

Ex-yacht: **OLIVIN**
120 tons: 122¾(pp) 124(oa) × 20 × 9¼d/6¾ feet:
two shafts, 8-cyl. Winton diesel engines (bore
8½″ × 12″ stroke) (B.H.P. not known) 13
knots, oil fuel: one 3-inch, two 5-inch (2 × 1)
guns: complement not known.

Ex-yacht: **SARD**
Not placed in service as armed yacht.

Ex-yacht: **IOLITE(i)**
Not placed in service as armed yacht.

Ex-yacht: **PHENAKITE**
360 tons: 183(oa) × 22½ × 9½ feet: two shafts,
7-cyl. Fairbanks Morse diesel engines (bore
14″ × 17″ stroke) B.H.P. 850 = 12½ knots, oil
fuel: one 3-inch, four ·5-inch (4 × 1) guns:
complement 40.

Ex-yacht: **CYMOPHANE**
523 tons: 148½(pp) 160¾(oa) × 26¼ × 13d/9¾
feet: two shafts, 6-cyl. Winton diesel engines
(bore 16½″ × 26″ stroke) (B.H.P. not known)
= 14 knots, oil fuel: one 3-inch A.A. two
·5-inch A.A. (2 × 1) guns: complement 49.

Ex-yacht: **COLLEEN**
230 tons: 139¾(pp) 150(oa) × 22½ × 10¼d/7½
feet: two shafts, 6-cyl. Winton diesel engines
(bore 14″ × 16″ stroke) (B.H.P. not known)
16 knots, oil fuel: one 3-inch gun:
complement not known.

Olivin
(ex-yacht *Bidou*)
Hull No: PYc.22

Launched:
1930

Built by: Bath I.W.

Transferred Maritime
Commission 23.10.46 for
disposal and scrapped.

Sard
(ex-yacht
Navigation)
Hull No: PYc.23

Launched:
unknown

Built by: unknown

U.S.C.G.
(WIX.338—1942), U.S.N.
YP.261 (1942).

Iolite(i)
(ex-yacht *Tara*)
Hull No: PYc.24

Launched:
unknown

Built by: unknown

YP.454 (1942).

Phenakite
(ex-yacht
Sachem)
Hull No: PYc.25

Launched:
1902

Built by: Pusey & Jones
(Wilmington)

Mercantile *Circle Line V*
(1946).

Cymophane
ex-yacht
Seaforth,
ex-*Robador*)
Hull No: PYc.26

Launched:
1926

Built by: Newport News

Transferred Maritime
Commission 10.6.48
for disposal.

Colleen
(ex-yacht *Colleen*)
Hull No: PYc.27

Launched:
1928

Built by: Pusey & Jones
(Wilmington)

U.S.C.G. (name
unchanged—1945).

Ability
(ex-yacht
Reomar IV,
ex-*Sylvia*)
Hull No: PYc.28

Launched:
1926

Built by: Defoe Boat &
Motor (Bay City)

Transferred Maritime
Commission 18.5.46 for
disposal.

Gallant
(ex-yacht *North
Star*, ex-*Falcon*,
ex-*Viking*)
Hull No: PYc.29

Launched:
1909

Built by: Pusey & Jones
(Wilmington)

Transferred War Shpg.
Admin. 28.6.45 for
disposal.

Vagrant
(ex-yacht
Vagrant)
Hull No: PYc.30

Launched:
6.13

Built by: Herreshoff
(Bristol)

Sold 1946.

Ex-yacht: **PALACE**
Not placed in service as armed yacht.

Ex-yacht: **BRAVE**
Not placed in service as armed yacht.

Ex-yacht: **FELICIA**
447 tons: $134\frac{3}{4}$(pp) $147\frac{3}{4}$(oa) $\times 24\frac{3}{4} \times 14\frac{1}{4}$d/$9\frac{1}{2}$
feet: two shafts, 8-cyl. Cooper-Bessemer diesel
engines (bore $9'' \times 12''$ stroke) and electric
motors (S.H.P. not known) 12 knots,
oil fuel: one 6-pounder gun: complement 42.

Ex-yacht: **PARAGON**
176 tons *gross*: 120(pp) $138\frac{1}{4}$(oa) $\times 19\frac{1}{4} \times 12$d/9
feet: two shafts, 6-cyl. Winton diesel engines
(bore $11'' \times 15''$ stroke) (B.H.P. not known)
14 knots, oil fuel: one 6-pounder, two
20mm A.A. (2×1) guns: complement not
known.

Ex-yacht: **MENTOR**
182 tons: $123\frac{3}{4}$(wl) $127\frac{1}{4}$(oa) $\times 21 \times \quad$ d/$6\frac{1}{4}$
feet: two shafts, diesel engines B.H.P. 600
= 12 knots, oil fuel: one 3-inch, two 20mm
A.A. (2×1) guns: complement 35.

Ex-yacht: **CAROLITA**
236 tons: 126(wl) $133\frac{3}{4}$(oa) $\times 23 \times 12\frac{1}{2}$d/$8\frac{1}{2}$
feet: two shafts, 6-cyl. Krupp diesel engines
(bore 330mm $\times$ 350mm stroke) (B.H.P. not
known) 14 knots, oil fuel: one 4-inch,
three·5-inch A.A. (3×1) guns: complement
not known.

Ex-yacht: **MARNELL**
180 tons: $125\frac{1}{2}$(wl) $\times 135$(oa) $\times 22\frac{3}{4} \times 10\frac{3}{4}$d/$6\frac{3}{4}$
feet: two shafts, 6-cyl. Cooper-Bessemer
diesel engines (bore $11'' \times 14''$ stroke)
(B.H.P. not known) = 14 knots, oil fuel:
one 4-inch, three ·5-inch A.A.(3×1) guns:
complement not known.

Ex-mercantile: **CAPTOR**
See under auxiliary minesweeper *Eagle* for
details.

Lash (ex-yacht Sylph *II* ex-*Stellaris*, ex-*Caroline*) *Launched:* 1914	*Built by:* Robert Jacob (City Island) Retroceded 18.5.45.	**Paragon** (ex-yacht *Paragon*) *Hull No:* PYc.36 *Launched:* 11.29	*Built by:* As above Transferred Maritime Commission 23.4.45 for disposal.
Tourist (ex-yacht *Tourist*) *Hull No:* PYc.32 *Launched:* unknown	*Built by:* .... YAG.14 (1942).	**Mentor** ex-yacht *Haida* *Hull No:* PYc.37 *Launched:* 1941	*Built by:* Robert Jacob (City Island) Woods Hole Oceanographic Ins. (1946–50); sold World Surplus Trading Co. (Honolulu) 19.5.42.
Palace (ex-mercantile *Palace*) *Hull No:* PYc.33 *Launched:* 1899	*Built by:* Delaware River Sbdg. (Chester) YAG.13 (1942).	**Carolita** (ex-yacht *Carolita*, ex-*Ripple*) *Hull No:* PYc.38 *Launched:* 1923	*Built by:* Germaniawerft (Kiel) Paid-off 28.2.44 and expended as target.
Brave (ex-yacht *Roseb*) *Hull No:* PYc.34 *Launched:* unknown YP.425 (1942).	*Built by:* unknown YP.425 (1942).	**Marnell** (ex-yacht *Marnell*) *Hull No:* PYc.39 *Launched:* 1930	*Built by:* Defoe Boat & Motor (Bay City) Transferred War Shpg. Admin. 30.4.47 for disposal.
Felicia (ex-yacht *Felicia*) *Hull No:* PYc.35 *Launched:* 9.31	*Built by:* Bath I.W. Transferred Maritime Commission 23.10.45 for disposal.	**Captor** (ex-*Eagle* ex-mercantile *Wave*, ex-*Harvard*) *Hull No:* PYc.40 *Launched:* 1938	*Built by:* Bethlehem (Quincy) Transferred War Shpg. Admin. 21.2.45 for disposal.

The yacht PARAGON *(29 Aug 1942) was armed with a 6pdr, two machine guns on the wheelhouse roof, and two 20mm A.A. (2× 1) guns aft.* PHOTOGRAPH: U.S. NAVY

Above: The yacht CAROLITA *(13 Nov 1942) was armed with a 4in gun forward and three ·5in A.A. (3× 1) machine guns. Below: The 3in gun aft has been removed from the yacht* PATRIOT *(13 Aug 1944).* PHOTOGRAPHS: U.S. NAVY

Iolite(ii)
(ex-yacht
Florence D)
Hull No: PYc.41

Launched:
1914

Built by: G. Lawley
(Neponset)

Internal explosion
Tomkinsville 26.8.44 and
written-off as constructive
total loss; transferred
Maritime Commission
1945 for disposal.

Leader
(ex-yacht *Curlew*)
Hull No: PYc.42

Launched:
8.27

Built by: Whites Yacht
(Southampton)

Yacht *Chito* (1949).

Sea Scout
(ex-yacht
Velero II)
Hull No: PYc.43

Launched:
1922

Built by: W. Muller
(Wilmington)

Retroceded 1944.

Perseverance
(ex-USCG
Bedford,
ex-*Condor*,
ex-*Corolus*,
ex-*Gipsy Jo*,
ex-*Athero*,
ex-*Gem*)
Hull No: PYc.44

Launched:
1913

Built by: G. Lawley
(Neponset)

Stricken 19.5.45 and
scrapped.

Black Douglas
(ex-USF & WLS
Black Douglas)
Hull No: PYc.45

Launched:
7.30

Built by: Bath I.W.

Retroceded Fish Wild Life
Service 1944.

Impetuous
(ex-*PC.454*,
ex-yacht *Arlis*,
ex-*Sybilla III*,
ex-*Paragon*)
Hull No: PYc.46

Launched:
1915

Built by: Robert Jacob
(City Island)

Transferred War Shpg.
Admin. 14.6.45 for
disposal.

Patriot
(ex-*PC.455*,
ex-yacht
Katoura)
Hull No: PYc.47

Launched:
1930

Built by: Herreshoff
(Bristol)

Transferred War Shpg.
Admin. 14.3.45 for
disposal.

Persistent
(ex-*PC.456*,
ex-yacht *Onwego*)
Hull No: PYc.48

Launched:
1931

Built by: New York Yacht
(Morris Heights)

Stricken 14.10.44.

Retort
(ex-*PC.458*,
ex-yacht
Evelyn R II,
ex-*Koogong*,
ex-*Enja IV*)
Hull No: PYc.49

Launched:
unknown

Built by: unknown

Retroceded 1944.

Sturdy
(ex-*PC.460*,
ex-yacht *Elda*,
ex-*Avalanche*)
Hull No: PYc.50

Launched:
1929

Built by: Consolidated
Sbdg. (Morris Heights)

Retroceded 1944.

Valiant
(ex-*PC.509*,
ex-yacht *Vara*)
Hull No: PYc.51

Launched:
1928

Built by: Herreshoff
(Bristol)

Retroceded 1944.

Venture
(ex-*PC.826*,
ex-yacht *Vixen*)
Hull No: PYc.52

Launched:
unknown

Built by: unknown

Sold 1945.

Machinery contracts: Sapphire, Andradite, Rhodolite, Ability, Felicia, Marnell, Captor, and *Black Douglas* engined by Cooper-Bessemer; *Amethyst, Agate, Onyx, Truant, Chalcedony, Jet, Albaster, Olivin, Cymophane, Colleen, Paragon, Seascout, Persistent,* and *Sturdy* by Winton; *Amber* by Atlas; *Aquamarine* and *Topaze* by Union Diesel; *Opal, Sardonyx, Garnet, Pyrope,* and *Carolita* by Krupp; *Phenakite* by Fairbanks Morse; *Gallant* by J. W. Sullivan; *Vagrant* re-engined by Speedway; *Lash* by Gas Engine & Power; *Leader* by Kromhout; *Valiant* by Trieber; *Moonstone* and *Perseverance* by builders; and *Emerald, Jasper, Peridot, Sard, Iolite(i). Tourist, Palace, Brave, Mentor, Iolite(ii), Impetuous, Patriot, Retort,* and *Venture* unknown.

Ex-yacht: **IOLITE(ii)**
200 tons: 154(oa) × 20 × 7½ feet: two shafts, diesel engines (B.H.P. not known) 10 knots, oil fuel: guns and complement not known.

Ex-yacht: **LEADER**
230 tons: 114¾(pp) 117(oa) × 19½ × 10½d/7 feet: two shafts, 4-cyl. Kromhout diesel engine (bore 300mm × 310mm stroke) (B.H.P. not known) 13 knots, oil fuel: two 20 mm A.A. (2 × 1) guns: complement 25.

Ex-yacht **SEA SCOUT**
195 tons *gross*: 118(wl) 125½(oa) × 20 × 10¾d/7 feet: two shafts, 6-cyl. Winton diesel engines (bore 7½″ × 11″ stroke) (B.H.P. and speed not known), oil fuel: guns and complement not known: wood hull.

Ex-yacht: **PERSEVERANCE**
190 tons: 153½(wl) 164½(oa) × 18 × 10d/7 feet: two w.t. boilers, two shafts, reciprocating (VTE—cyl. 12⅜″: 19″: 28″ = 15″ stroke) (I.H.P. not known) 18 knots, oil fuel: one 20mm A.A. gun: complement 22.

Ex-yacht: **BLACK DOUGLAS**
371 tons *gross*: 118(wl) 153(oa) × 32 × 17½d/12 feet: two shafts, 8-cyl. Cooper-Bessemer diesel engines (bore 9″ × 12″ stroke) (B.H.P. and speed not known), oil fuel: guns and complement not known: rigged as 3-masted schooner.

Ex-yacht: **IMPETUOUS**
140 tons: 121(oa) × 6 feet: two shafts, diesel engines B.H.P. 600 = 16 knots, oil fuel: six ·3-inch (2 × 2 and 2 × 1) guns: complement not known.

Ex-yacht: **PATRIOT**
83 tons: 96½(oa) × 16½ × 6 feet: two shafts, petrol engines B.H.P. 850 = 18 knots, gasoline fuel: one 3-inch, two ·3-inch (2 × 1) guns: complement not known: wood hull.

Ex-yacht: **PERSISTENT**
110 tons: 119(wl) 120(oa) × 22 × 11d/6½ feet: two shafts, 8-cyl. Winton diesel engines (bore 8″ × 10″ stroke) (B.H.P. not known) = 12 knots, oil fuel: four ·3-inch (4 × 1) guns: complement not known: wood hull.

Ex-yacht: **RETORT**
164 tons *gross*: 120(oa) × 20 × 7½ feet: one boiler, two shafts, turbines S.H.P. 450 (speed not known): oil fuel: guns and complement not known.

Ex-yacht: **STURDY**
373 tons *gross*: 153(wl) 154(oa) × 24 × 12½d/8 feet: two shafts, 6-cyl. Winton diesel engines (bore 14″ × 16″ stroke) B.H.P. 1,500 (speed not known): oil fuel: guns and complement not known.

Ex-yacht: **VALIANT**
356 tons *gross*: 149(wl) 150(oa) × 24 × 13¼d/8 feet: two shafts, 12-cyl. Trieber diesel engines (bore 9″ × 12″ stroke) B.H.P. 1,500 (speed not known): oil fuel: guns and complement not known.

Ex-yacht: **VENTURE**
No details available.

"Lapwing" class:

Bittern, Bobalink, Brant, Cormorant, Finch, Grebe, Kingfisher, Lark, Oriole, Owl, Partridge, Penguin, Quail, Rail, Robin, Seagull, Tanager, Tern, Turkey, Vireo, Whippoorwill, Woodcock.

The design of this class was hurriedly prepared during the First World War to provide the United States Navy with their first custom-built minesweepers (AM), and to expedite delivery their design—perhaps mistakenly—was cast about the mercantile tug. In consequence they proved better tugs than minesweepers, and as they were more often employed in the former role during the inter-war years this rather restricted naval development with minesweeping techniques.

Of the fifty-four units (AM.1–54) originally comprising this class five were cancelled in 1919, five were lost before the outbreak of the Second World War, and siz were transferred to other U.S. Government departments; and six were converted to submarine rescue vessels (ASR) in 1929, nine to seaplane tenders (AVP) in 1939, and one to gate vessel (YNG). The six units in Government service were re-aquired in 1941 but were adapted as salvage vessels (ARS); and as they were only able to operate wire sweeps all surviving minesweepers—five had already become war losses—were reclassified as tugs (AT) in 1942.

The "Lapwing" class was rigged with two pole masts, and the foremast—which was originally stepped forward of the bridge—was re-stepped abaft the bridge in most units during the war, and in some two 20mm A.A. (2 × 1) guns replaced the after 3in gun. A short derrick was arranged on the fore side of the mainmast, and a long derrick on the after side to handle sweep gear.

DISPLACEMENT: 950 tons (1,250 tons full load).
DIMENSIONS: 174(wl) 187¾(oa) × 35½ × 9¾ (12 full load) feet.
MACHINERY: Two Babcock & Wilcox boilers; one shaft, reciprocating (VTE—cyl. 19″ : 29″ : 46″ × 30″ stroke) I.H.P. 1,400 = 14 knots.
BUNKERS: O.F. 275 tons.
ARMAMENT: Two 3-inch/50cal (2 × 1), three ·5-inch A.A. (3 × 1) guns.
COMPLEMENT: 78.

Owl
Hull No: AM.2
Launched: 4.3.18
Built by: Todd (Brooklyn)
AT.137 (1942), ATO.137 (1944); sold Pacific Metal & Salvage (Nordland) 27.6.47 and scrapped.

Finch
Hull No: AM.9
Launched: 30.3.18
Built by: Standard Sbdg. (New York)
Bombed Japanese aircraft Corregidor 9.4.42 and foundered following day, salved and I.J.N. patrol boat No.103 (1943); bombed U.S.N. aircraft south-west Cape Padaran 12.1.45.

Robin
Hull No: AM.3
Launched: 17.6.18
Built by: As above
AT.140 (1942), ATO.140 (1940); sold 2.48 and scrapped.

Tanager
Hull No: AM.5
Launched: 2.3.18
Built by: Staten Island Sbdg.
Gunfire Japanese shore batteries off Corregidor 4.5.42.

Turkey
Hull No: AM.13
Launched: 30.4.18
Built by: As above
AT.143 (1942), ATO.143 (1944); transferred Maritime Commission 12.46 for disposal.

Oriole
Hull No: AM.7
Launched: 3.7.18
Built by: As above
AT.136 (1942), ATO.136 (1944); sold M. E. Baker (Suisun Bay) 6.1.47.

Woodcock
Hull No: AM.14
Launched: 12.5.18
Built by: Chester Sbdg.
AT.145 (1942), ATO.145 (1944); sold 1.48 and scrapped.

High-speed minesweepers: DMS.1–42

These vessels were converted from destroyers to serve as high-speed minesweepers for fleet operations in areas where an offensive sweep would be open to attack from enemy warships, aircraft, or shore batteries. They therefore retained most of their defensive gun armament while sacrificing all of the offensive torpedo armament to accommodate wire and LL sweep gear. In 1940 eighteen old destroyers of the "Wickes"/"Clemson" classes were converted to this role (DMS.1–18), to be followed by twenty-four "Bristol" class (DMS.19–42) in 1944. Full details of these vessels were given in the companion volume *American Fleet and Escort Destroyers*.

Quail(i)
Hull No: AM.15

Launched:
6.10.18

Built by: As above

Bombed Japanese aircraft and scuttled off Corregidor 5.5.42.

Partridge(i)
Hull No: AM.16

Launched:
15.10.18

Built by: Chester Sbdg.

AT.138 (1942), ATO.138 (1944); torpedoed German MTB off Normandy 11.6.44.

Bobolink
Hull No: AM.20

Launched:
15.6.18

Built by: Baltimore Sbdg.

AT.131 (1942), ATO.131 (1944); transferred Maritime Commission 5.10.46 for disposal.

Seagull
Hull No: AM.30

Launched:
24.12.18

Built by: Gas Engine & Power (Morris Heights)

AT.141 (1942), ATO.141 (1944); sold 4.47 and scrapped.

Bittern(i)
Hull No: AM.36

Launched:
15.2.19

Built by: As above

Bombed Japanese aircraft Cavite 10/12.41.

Lark
Hull No: AM.21

Launched:
6.8.18

Built by: As above

AT.168 (1942), ATO.168 (1944); sold 1.47 and scrapped.

Tern
Hull No: AM.31

Launched:
22.3.19

Built by: As above

AT.142 (1942), ATO.142 (1944); sold 7.47 and scrapped.

Cormorant
Hull No: AM.40

Launched:
5.2.19

Built by: Todd (Brooklyn)

AT.133 (1942), ATO.133 (1944); sold 3.47 and scrapped.

Brant
AM.24

Launched:
30.5.18

Built by: Sun Sbdg. (Chester)

AT.132 (1942), ARS.32 (1942); transferred Maritime Commission 19.8.46 for disposal.

Penguin
Hull No: AM.33

Launched:
12.6.18

Built by: New Jersey D.D. (Elizabethport)

Bombed Japanese aircraft off Guam 8.12.41.

Grebe
Hull No: AM.43

Launched:
17.12.18

Built by: Staten Island Sbdg.

AT.134 (1942); wrecked south of Fiji 5.12.42.

Kingfisher
Hull No: AM.25

Launched:
30.3.18

Built by: Puget Sound N.Y.

AT.135 (1942), ATO.135 (1944); sold M. E. Baker (Suisun Bay) 3.6.47.

Whippoorwill
Hull No: AM.35

Launched:
28.1.19

Built by: Alabama D.D. (Mobile)

AT.169 (1942), ATO.169 (1944); transferred Maritime Commission 11.46 for disposal.

Vireo
Hull No: AM.52

Launched:
26.5.19

Built by: Philadelphia N.Y.

AT.144 (1942), ATO.144 (1944); sold 2.47 and scrapped.

Rail
Hull No: AM.26

Launched:
25.4.18

Built by: As above

AT.139 (1942), ATO.139 (1944); sold 1.47 and scrapped.

Machinery contracts: All engined by Harlan & Hollingsworth.

31

"Raven" class.

Osprey, Raven

These vessels were authorised in 1938 as prototypes for a new series of minesweepers to replace the "Lapwing" class which had been ordered 20 years earlier, and those replacement was long overdue. The adoption of diesel main propulsion—with its attendant economies—was an innovation for American surface warships which proved successful, and as a result of British war experience the capability of these prototypes was extended to cope with influence as well as the conventional moored mine.

On a reduced tonnage the *Raven* was a marked improvement on the *Lapwing*: a raised fo'c'sle improved seaworthiness, increased speed permitted a faster passage to and from operational areas and enabled her to double as an A/S vessel if required, and while length is not the most desirable feature of a minesweeper it was only moderately increased and enabled sea speed to be easier maintained. An adequate A.A. armament of two 3in (2 × 1 forward and aft) and four 20mm A.A. (4 × 1 amidships) was provided together with sonar, depth charges, and wire and LL sweep gear.

In all respects the *Raven* compared favourably with any contemporary minesweeper, and was distinctively rigged with two funnels and a pole foremast. Boats stowed between the funnels were handled by a derrick stepped from the foremast.

Below: As completed the OSPREY *(26 May 1941) had 3in A.A. guns forward and aft controlled by a pedestal director over the wheelhouse, and only a single A.A. machine gun between the funnels. Bottom: The* RAVEN *(20 Sep 1942) had four 20mm A.A. (4 × 1) guns added over the wheelhouse and between the funnels.*
PHOTOGRAPHS: U.S. NAVY

DISPLACEMENT: 810 tons (1,040 tons full load).
DIMENSIONS: 215(wl) 220½(oa) × 32¼ × 8½ (9¼ full load) feet.
MACHINERY: Two shafts: Fairbanks More diesel engines B.H.P. 1,800 = 17 knots.
BUNKERS: O.F. 200 tons.
ARMAMENT: Two 3-inch A.A. (2 × 1), four 20mm A.A. (4 × 1) guns.
COMPLEMENT: 105.

Raven   *Built by:* Norfolk N.Y.
Hull No: AM.55

     MSF.55 (1955); stricken
Launched: 1967 and scrapped.
24.8.40

Osprey(i)   *Built by:* As above
Hull No: AM.56

     Mined off Normandy
Launched: 5.6.44.
24.8.40

Machinery contracts: Engined by Fairbanks Morse.

DISPLACEMENT: 890 tons (1,250 tons full load).
DIMENSIONS: 215(wl) 221¾(oa) × 32¼ × 9½
(10¾ full load) feet.
MACHINERY: Two shafts; 12-cylinder General
Motors (bore 8½″ × 10″ stroke) except
AM.57–65 ALCO, *AM.100–111* Busch-
Sulzer, and *AM.314–320* and *340* Baldwin
diesel engines and electric motors
B.H.P. 3,532 except *AM.57–65 & 100–111*
B.H.P. 3,118 and *AM.314–320 & 340*
B.H.P. 2,976 = 18 knots.
BUNKERS: O.F. 325 tons.
ARMAMENT: Two 3-inch/50cal A.A. (2 × 1) and
four 20mm A.A. (4 × 1) except *AM.314* up
one 3-inch/50cal A.A., two 40mm A.A.
(2 × 1), six (*AM.314–324, 340* and *341*)/eight
(*AM.371–390*) 20mm A.A. (6/8 × 1) guns.
COMPLEMENT: 105 except *AM.371–390* 117.

Auk
Hull No: AM.57   *Built by:* Norfolk N.Y.

Launched: MSF.57 (1955); stricken
26.8.41   1.8.59 and scrapped.

Broadbill   *Built by:* Defoe Sbdg.
Hull No: AM.58   (Bay City)

Launched: MSF.58 (1955); stricken
21.5.42   1.7.72.

Chickadee   *Built by:* As above
Hull No: AM.59
                      MSF.59 (1955),
Launched: Uruguayan Navy
20.7.42   *Comandante Pedro
                      Campbell* (1966).

Nuthatch
Hull No: AM.60   *Built by:* As above

Launched: MSF.60 (1955); expended
16.9.42   as target off Southern
                      California . . .12.67.

Pheasant
Hull No: AM.61   *Built by:* As above

Launched: MSF.61 (1955); stricken
24.10.42   1.12.66 and expended as
                      target.

Shelldrake
Hull No: AM.62   *Built by:* General
                      Engineering (Alameda)
Launched:
12.2.42   AGS.19 (1952); stricken
                      30.6.68 and scrapped.

Skylark
Hull No: AM.63   *Built by:* As above

Launched: Mined off Okinawa
12.3.42   28.3.45.

"Auk" class:

Ardent, Auk, Broadbill, Champion, Chickadee, Chief, Competent, Defense, Devastator, Dextrous, Gladiator, Heed, Herald, Impeccable, Minivet, Motive, Murrelet, Nuthatch, Oracle, Peregrine, Pheasant, Pigeon, Pilot, Pioneer, Pochard, Portent, Prevail, Ptarmigan, Pursuit, Quail, Redstart, Requisite, Revenge, Roselle, Ruddy, Sage, Scoter, Seer, Sentinel, Shelldrake, Shoveller, Skill, Skylark, Spear, Speed, Sprig, Staff, Starling, Steady, Strive, Surfbird, Sustain, Swallow, Sway, Swerve, Swift, Symbol, Tanager, Tercel, Threat, Tide, Token, Toucan, Towee, Triumph, Tumult, Usage, Velocity, Vigilance, Vital, Waxwing, Wheatear, Zeal, and **Twenty** units for the Royal Navy.

Before even the prototypes *Raven* and *Osprey* could be fully evaluated the U.S.A. was drawn into the Second World War, and a crash programme of navel construction naturally followed. However, sufficient experience had already been obtained with the *Raven* to embark on a large-scale production series, and prior to the American entry into the war the Royal Navy had placed an order for thirty-two of these units (BAM.1–32).

To energise her LL sweep the *Raven* was fitted with diesel generators, but it was immediately apparent that diesel-electric propulsion would provide a superior alternative to a geared diesel drive as, when not engaged in sweeping, the generators could be utilised to provide additional power for the propulsion electric motors, and therefore boost free-route speed. This significant innovation was incorporated into the production series—the "Auk" class—and permitted considerable operational flexibility at little extra cost except for a slight increase in displacement. The United States Navy was particularly fortunate in that it was backed by the industrial capacity to install diesel-electric propulsion on a large scale, and therefore was not inhibited in its approach to an optimum design. In the U.K., for example, the type of machinery available for main propulsion in any quantity was very circumscribed, and consequently British designs had to be modified to accept what was available rather than install what was desirable.

From the *Champion* (AM.314) onwards the after 3in A.A. was replaced by two 40mm A.A. (2 × 1) guns, and from the *Minivet* (AM.371) four additional 20mm A.A. (4 × 1) were added amidships and on the quarterdeck, while some units later shipped twin mountings in place of the single 40mm A.A. guns. SW.RDF was added at the masthead in the earlier units and was built-in to the later vessels.

The AUK − *lead ship of her class* − *as completed (20 June 1943) with two 3in A.A. (2 × 1) and four 20mm A.A. (4 × 1) guns, and SW.RDF fitted at the masthead.*   PHOTOGRAPH: U.S. NAVY

The "Auk" class performed admirable war service, but—in common with all steel-hulled minesweepers—their invulnerability to influence mines decreased as the war progressed owing to the increased sensitivity and sophistication applied to magnetic mines; and by the close of the war only wood-hulled minesweepers could be risked in such fields.

Of the thirty-two units ordered by the Royal Navy, twelve were retained by the United States Navy but the remaining twenty—plus two additional vessels from the American programme—were transferred as planned.

In the CHAMPION *(13 Oct 1943) the after 3in A.A. has been replaced by two 40mm A.A. (2 × 1) guns, two more 20mm A.A. (2 × 1) guns were added between the funnels, and AW and SW.RDF fitted at the masthead.*
PHOTOGRAPH: U.S. NAVY

Starling
Hull No: AM.64   *Built by:* As above

Launched: MSF.64 (1955); stricken
11.4.42   1.7.72.

Swallow
Hull No: AM.65   *Built by:* As above

Launched: Bombed Japanese aircraft
6.5.42   off Okinawa 22.4.45.

Heed
Hull No: AM.100   *Built by:* General
Engineering (Alameda)

Launched:
19.6.42   MSF.100 (1955); stricken
1.3.67 and scrapped.

Herald
Hull No: AM.101   *Built by:* As above

Launched: MSF.101 (1955); stricken
4.7.42   1.7.72.

Motive
Hull No: AM.102   *Built by:* As above

Launched: MSF.102 (1955); expended
17.8.42   as target 1968.

Oracle
Hull No: AM.103   *Built by:* As above

Launched: MSF.103 (1955); stricken
30.9.42   1.12.66 and expended as
target.

Pilot
Hull No: AM.104   *Built by:* Pennsylvania
Shyd. (Beaumont)

Launched:
5.7.42   MSF.104 (1955); stricken
1.7.72.

Pioneer
Hull No: AM.105   *Built by:* As above

Launched: MSF.105 (1955); stricken
26.7.42   1.7.72.

Portent
Hull No: AM.106   *Built by:* As above

Launched: Mined off Anzio 22.1.44.
16.8.42

Prevail
Hull No: AM.107   *Built by:* As above

Launched: AGS.20 (1952); sold
13.9.42   Union Minerals & Alloys
(New York) 10.1.64 and
scrapped.

Pursuit
Hull No: AM.108   *Built by:* Winslow Marine
(Seattle)

Launched: AGS.17 (1952); stricken
12.6.42   1.7.60 and scrapped.

Requisite
Hull No: AM.109   *Built by:* Winslow Marine
(Seattle)

Launched: AGS.18 (1952); stricken
25.7.42   1964 and scrapped.

Revenge
(ex-*Right*)   *Built by:* As above
Hull No: AM.110

Launched: MSF.110 (1955); sold
7.11.42   Peck Iron & Metal Co.
6.10.67 and scrapped.

Sage
Hull No: AM.111   *Built by:* As above

Launched: MSF.111 (1955); stricken
21.11.42   1.7.72.

Seer
Hull No: AM.112   *Built by:* American Sbdg.
(Lorain)

Launched: MSF.112 (1955), MMC.5
23.5.42   (1960), R.N.N. *Uller*
(1960).

Sentinel(i)
Hull No: AM.113   *Built by:* American Sbdg.
(Lorain)

Launched: Bombed German aircraft
4.6.42   off Licata 12.7.43.

The MOTIVE *(24 May 1944) was armed and equipped as the* CHAMPION *(opposite): note that only one boat is carried (to starboard) abreast the fore funnel.*   PHOTOGRAPH: U.S. NAVY

35

Staff		Speed		Steady	
Hull No: AM.114	Built by: As above	Hull No: AM.116	Built by: American Sbdg. (Cleveland)	Hull No: AM.118	Built by: As above
Launched: 17.6.42	MSF.114 (1955); sold Southern Scrap Materials (New Orleans) 17.11.67 and scrapped.	Launched: 18.4.42	MSF.116 (1955), South Korean Navy *Sunchon* (1967).	Launched: 6.6.42	MSF.118 (1955), Chinese Navy (Nationalist) *Ping Ching* (1968).

Skill		Strive		Sustain	
Hull No: AM.115	Built by: As above	Hull No: AM.117	Built by: As above	Hull No: AM.119	Built by: American Sbdg. (Cleveland)
Launched: 22.6.42	Torpedoed German submarine *U.593* south of Capri 25.9.43.	Launched: 16.5.42	MSF.117 (1955), MMC.1 (1959), R.N.N. *Gar* (1959).	Launched: 23.6.42	MSF.119 (1955), MMC.2 (1959), R.N.N. *Tyr* (1959)

Sway
Hull No: AM.120

Built by: John H. Mathis (Camden)

Launched: 29.9.42

MSF.120 (1955).

Below: The DEFENSE *(30 Sep 1945) and the* SCOTER *(bottom – 13 Apr 1945): the former temporarily lacks all 20mm A.A. guns.* PHOTOGRAPHS: U.S. NAVY

Swerve
Hull No: AM.121

Built by: As above.

Launched: 25.2.43

Mined off Anzio 9.7.44.

Swift
Hull No: AM.122

Built by: As above

Launched: 5.12.42

MSF.122 (1955); stricken 1.7.72.

Symbol
Hull No: AM.123

Built by: Savannah

Launched: 2.7.42

MSF.123 (1955); stricken 1.7.72.

Threat
Hull No: AM.124

Built by: As above

Launched: 15.8.42

MSF.124 (1955); stricken 1.7.72.

Tide

Built by: As above

Launched: 7.9.42

Mined off Normandy 7.6.44.

Token
Hull No: AM.126

Built by: Gulf Sbdg. (Madisonville)

Launched: 28.3.42

MSF.126 (1955); sold Southern Scrap Materials (New Orleans) 17.11.67 and scrapped.

Tumult
Hull No: AM.127

Built by: As above

Launched: 19.4.42

MSF.127 (1955); stricken 1967 and scrapped.

Velocity
Hull No: AM.128

Launched:
19.4.42

Built by: As above

MSF.128 (1955); stricken 1.7.72.

Vital
Hull No: AM.129
Launched:
7.9.42

Built by: As above

R.N. *Strenuous* (1943), mercantile *Evening Star* (1948), *Pride of the West* (1949); sold incomplete Walter Ritscher, arrived Hamburg 7.56 and scrapped.

Usage
Hull No: AM.130

Launched:
4.10.42

Built by: As above

R.N. *Tourmaline* (1943); sold 1.47.

Zeal
Hull No: AM.131

Launched:
15.9.42

Built by: As above

MSF.131 (1955); stricken 1967 and scrapped.

Unnamed
Hull No:
AM.314–320

Built by: unknown

See BAM.1–7.

Overseer
Hull No: AM.321

Built by: unknown

See BAM.16.

Unnamed
Hull No:
AM.322–324

Built by: unknown

See BAM.22–24.

Unnamed
Hull No: AM.340

Built by: unknown

See BAM.8.

Unnamed
Hull No: AM.341

Built by: unknown

See BAM.30.

Minivet
Hull No: AM.371

Launched:
8.11.44

Built by: Savannah Machine

Mined Tsushima Strait 29.12.45.

Murrelet
Hull No: AM.372

Launched:
29.12.44

Built by: As above

MSF.372 (1955), Philippine Navy *Rizal* (1965).

Peregrine
Hull No: AM.373

Launched:
17.2.45

Built by: As above

MSF.373 (1945), AG.164 (1964); stricken 1.2.69 and scrapped.

Pigeon
Hull No: AM.374
Launched:
28.3.45

Built by: As above

MSF.374 (1955); sold Peck Iron & Metal (Portsmouth, Va.) 6.10.67 and scrapped.

Pochard
Hull No: AM.375

Launched:
11.6.44

Built by: As above

MSF.375 (1955); sold Southern Scrap Materials (New Orleans) 17.11.67 and scrapped.

Ptarmigan
Hull No: AM.376

Launched:
15.7.44

Built by: As above

MSF.376 (1955), South Korean Navy *Shin Song* (1963).

Quail(ii)
Hull No: AM.377

Launched:
20.8.44

Built by: As above

MSF.377 (1955); sold Southern Scrap Materials

(New Orleans) 17.11.67 and scrapped.

Redstart
Hull No: AM.378

Launched:
18.10.44

Built by: As above

MSF.378 (1955), Chinese Navy (Nationalist) *Wu Sheng* (1965).

Roselle
Hull No: AM.379

Launched:
29.8.44

Built by: As above

MSF.379 (1955); stricken 1.7.72.

Ruddy
Hull No: AM.380

Launched:
29.10.44

Built by: Gulf Sbdg. (Madisonville)

MSF.380 (1955), Peruvian Navy *Galvez* (1960).

Scoter
Hull No: AM.381

Launched:
26.9.44

Built by: As above

MSF.381 (1955); stricken 1.7.72.

Shoveller
Hull No: AM.382

Launched:
10.12.44

Built by: As above

MSF.382 (1955), Peruvian Navy *Diez Canseco* (1960).

Surfbird
Hull No: AM.383

Launched:
31.8.44

Built by: American Sbdg. (Lorain)

MSF.383(1955), ADG.383 (1957).

Sprig
Hull No: AM.384
Launched:
15.9.44

Built by: As above

MSF.384 (1955); stricken 1.7.72.

Tanager(ii)
Hull No: AM.385

Launched:
9.12.44

Built by: As above

MSF.385 (1955), U.S.C.G (WTR.385—1963).

Tercel
Hull No: AM.386

Launched:
16.12.44

Built by: As above

MSF.386 (1955); stricken 1.7.72.

Toucan
Hull No: AM.387

Launched:
15.9.44

Built by: American Sbdg. (Cleveland)

MSF.387 (1955), Chinese Navy (Nationalist) *Chein Men* (1964); gunfire of Chinese Navy (Communist) warships south of Quemoy 6/8/55.

Towhee
Hull No: AM.388

Launched:
6.1.45

Built by: As above

MSF.388 (1955), AGS.28 (1964); stricken 1.5.69 and scrapped.

Waxwing
Hull No: AM.389

Launched:
10.3.45

Built by: American Sbdg. (Cleveland)

MSF389 (1955), Chinese Navy (Nationalist) *Chu Yung* (1965).

Wheater
Hull No: AM.390

Launched:
21.4.45

Built by: As above

MSF.390 (1955); stricken 1.7.72.

Machinery contracts: All engined by General Motors except AM.57–65 by ALCO, AM.100–111 by Busch-Sulzer, and AM.314–320 and 340 by Baldwin (diesel engines).

Wire sweep gear was omitted from the stern of the SURFBIRD *(3 May 1945) and two additional 20mm A.A. (2 × 1) guns mounted instead.*   PHOTOGRAPH: U.S. NAVY

Akbar
Hull No: BAM.1

Launched:

Built by: General Engineering (Alameda)

Champion (AM.314), MSF.314 (1955); stricken 1.7.72.

Alice
Hull No: BAM.2

Launched:
5.1.43

Built by: As above

Chief (AM.315), MSF.315 (1955); stricken 1.7.72.

Amelia
Hull No: BAM.3

Launched:
9.1.43

Built by: As above

Competent (AM.316), MSF.316 (1955); stricken 1.7.72.

Amity
Hull No: BAM.4

Launched:
18.2.43

Built by: As above

Defence (AM.317), MSF.317 (1955); stricken 1.7.72.

Augusta
Hull No: BAM.5

Launched:
19.4.43

Built by: As above

Devastator (AM.318), MSF.318 (1955); stricken 1.7.72.

Blaze
Hull No: BAM.6

Launched:
7.5.43

Built by: As above

Gladiator (AM.319), MSF.319 (1955); stricken 1.7.72.

Brutus
Hull No: BAM.7

Launched:
21.5.43

Built by: As above

Impeccable (AM.320), MSF.320 (1955); stricken 1.7.72.

Buffalo
Hull No: BAM.8

Launched:
22.6.43

Built by: As above

Ardent (AM.340), MSF.340 (1955); stricken 1.7.72.

Catherine
Hull No: BAM.9

Launched:
7.9.42

Built by: Associated Sbdr. (Seattle)

Turkish Navy *Erdemli* (1947).

Cato
Hull No:
BAM.10

Launched:
7.9.42

Built by: As above

Torpedoed German 'Marder' off Normandy 6.7.44.

Celerity
Hull No:
BAM.11

Launched:
20.6.43

Built by: As above

R.N. *Pique* (1943), Turkish Navy *Eregli* (1947).

Chamois
Hull No:
BAM.12

Launched:
26.10.42

Built by: As above

Mined off Normandy 21.7.44 and written-off as constructive total loss, mercantile *Morning Star* (1948); sold Walter Ritscher, arrived Hamburg . . .7.56 and scrapped.

Chance
Hull No:
BAM.13

Launched:
26.10.42

Built by: As above

Turkish Navy *Edremit* (1947).

Combatant
Hull No:
BAM.14

Launched:
27.11.42

Built by: As above

Sold 24.12.46.

Cynthia
Hull No:
BAM.15

Launched:
25.1.43

Built by: As above

Sold 16.12.47.

Elfreda
(ex-USN *Overseer*)
Hull No:
BAM.16

Launched:
25.1.43

Built by: As above

Turkish Navy *Cesmi* (1947).

Gazelle
Hull No:
BAM.17

Launched:
10.1.43

Built by: Savannah Mackine

Sold 17.7.47.

The SPRIG *(3 MAY 1945) with two additional 20mm A.A. (2× 1) guns aft in place of wire sweep gear.*
PHOTOGRAPH: U.S. NAVY

Gorgon
Hull No:
BAM.18

Launched:
24.1.43

Built by: Savannah
Machine

Sold 24.12.46.

Grecian
Hull No:
BAM.19

Launched:
10.3.43

Built by: As above

Turkish Navy *Edincik*
(1947).

Magic
Hull No:
BAM.20

Launched:
24.5.43

Built by: As above

Torpedoed German
'Marder' off Normandy
6.7.44.

Pylades
Hull No:
BAM.21

Launched:
27.6.43

Built by: As above

Torpedoed German
'Marder' off Normandy
8.7.44.

Errant
Hull No:
BAM.22

Launched:
25.2.43

Built by: Associated Sbdr.
(Seattle)

Spear (AM.322), MSF.322
(1955); stricken 1.7.72.

Espoir
Hull No:
BAM.23

Launched:
25.2.43

Built by: As above

Triumph (AM.323),
MSF.323 (1955), MMC.3
(1960), R.N.N. *Brage*
(1961).

Exploit
Hull No:
BAM.24

Launched:
5.4.43

Built by: As above

Vigilance (AM.324),
MSF.324 (1955),
Philippino Navy *Quezon*
(1967).

Fairy
Hull No:
BAM.25

Launched:
5.4.43

Built by: As above

Sold 26.8.47.

Floriziel
Hull No:
BAM.26

Launched:
20.5.43

Built by: As above

Mercantile *Aida* (1947).

Foam
Hull No:
BAM.27

Launched:
20.5.43

Built by: As above

Sold 26.8.47.

Frolic
Hull No:
BAM.38

Launched:
22.7.43

Built by: As above

Turkish Navy *Candarli*
(1947).

Garnet
Hull No:
BAM.29

Launched:
20.6.43

Built by: As above

R.N. *Jasper* (1943),
mercantile *Pandelis* (1946);
sold Brodospas (Split)
5.68 and scrapped.

Sepoy
Hull No:
BAM.30

Launched:
17.1.43

Built by: Gulf Sbdg.
(Chickasaw)

Dextrous (AM.341),
MSF.341 (1955), South
Korean Navy *Koje* (1967).

Steadfast
Hull No:
BAM.31

Launched-
17.1.43

Built by: As above

Sold 24.12.46.

Tattoo
Hull No:
BAM.32

Launched:
27.1.43

Built by: As above

Turkish Navy *Carsamba*
(1947).

Machinery contracts: All engined by General
Motors except *first eight* by Baldwin (diesel
engines).

Auxiliary Minesweepers

As with gunboats the extreme shortage of minesweepers resulted in twenty trawlers and forty-two purse seiners/draggers being acquired in 1940–41 as a temporary measure. The trawlers were all deep-sea vessels of steel construction and were fitted for wire sweeping only, while the seiners and draggers were all coastal craft of wooden construction but were fitted for both wire and LL sweeping.

The conversion of two trawlers—the *Goldcrest(i)* and the *Eagle*—was not finally implemented, and they were reclassed as armed yachts (PYc) and renamed: the latter serving as a decoy ship. Most of the remaining trawlers were relegated to subsidiary duties, or paid-off, by 1944, when superseded by war-built minesweepers, and several were re-classified as miscellaneous auxiliaries (IX).

Below: Auxiliary minesweeper BULLFINCH *(30 May 1943) was armed with a 3in gun forward and two A.A. (2 × 1) machine guns over the wheelhouse. Bottom: Auxiliary minesweeper* BLUEBIRD *(20 Jan 1942).*
PHOTOGRAPHS: U.S. NAVY

Ex-mercantile: **BULLFINCH, CARDINAL**
425 tons: 124½(pp) 136¼(oa) × 24 × 9 (11 full load) feet: one shaft, 7-cyl. Fairbanks Morse diesel engine (bore 14″ × 17″ stroke) B.H.P. 735 = 10 knots, oil fuel: one 3-inch/50cal gun: complement not known.

Ex-mercantile: **CATBIRD-CURLEW**
570 tons: 137¾(pp) 147¾(oa) × 25¼ × 12 (full load) feet: one shaft, 5-cyl. Fairbanks Morse diesel engine (bore 14″ × 17″ stroke) B.H.P. 575 = 10½ knots, oil fuel: one 3-inch/23cal (*Catbird*) or 3-inch/50cal (*Curlew*) gun: complement not known.

Ex-mercantile: **FLICKER**
510 tons: 138½(pp) 147½(oa) × 25 × 12 (full load) feet: one shaft, 7-cyl. Fairbanks Morse diesel engine (bore 14″ × 17″ stroke) B.H.P. 735 = 11 knots, oil fuel: one 3-inch/23cal gun: complement not known.

Bullfinch(i)
ex-mercantile
Villanova)
Hull No: AM.66

Launched:
12.10.37

Built by: Bath I.W

Transferred Maritime
Commission 28.7.45 for
disposal.

Catbird
(ex-mercantile
Bittern)
Hull No: AM.68

Launched:
1938

Built by: Charleston

IX.183 (1944), mercantile
Salhus (1947).

Flicker(i)
(ex-mercantile
Delaware)
Hull No: AM.70

Launched:
1937

Built by: Bath I.W.

IX.165 (1944), mercantile
Delware (45).

Cardina(i)
(ex-mercantile
Jeanne d'Arc)
Hull No: AM.67

Launched:
10.37

Built by: As above

Transferred Maritime
Commission 29.8.45
for disposal.

Curlew
(ex-mercantile
Kittiwake)
Hull No: AM.69

Launched:
1937

Built by: As above

IX.170 (1944), mercantile
Ragon (1946).

Albatross(i)
(ex-mercantile
Illinois)
Hull No: AM.71

Launched:
19.3.31

Built by: As above

IX.171 (1944); transferred
Maritime Commission
15.11.45 for disposal.

Below: Auxiliary minesweepers CATBIRD *(29 Sep 1941) and* CURLEW *(bottom – 16 May 1941).*
PHOTOGRAPHS: U.S. NAVY

Ex-mercantile: **ALBATROSS, BLUEBIRD**
465 tons: 121½(pp) 132½(oa) × 24 × 12 (full load) feet: one shaft, 6-cyl. Fairbanks Morse diesel engine (bore 14″ × 17″ stroke) B.H.P. 630 = 10½ knots, oil fuel: one 3-inch/50cal, two machine (2 × 1) guns: complement not known.

Ex-mercantile: **GRACKLE**
455 tons: 122¼(pp) 132½(oa) × 24 × 11½ (full load) feet: one shaft, 6-cyl. Cooper-Bessemer diesel engine (bore 16″ × 20″ stroke) B.H.P. 510 = 10 knots, oil fuel: one 3-inch/50cal gun: complement not known.

Ex-mercantile: **GULL**
410 tons: 114(pp) 124¼(oa) × 23 × 10¾ (11½ full load) feet: one shaft, 6-cyl. Cooper-Bessemer diesel engine (bore 14″ × 17″ stroke) B.H.P. 390 = 10 knots, oil fuel: one 3-inch/50cal gun: complement not known.

Ex-mercantile: **KITE, LINNET**
410 tons: 114¾(pp) 123¾(oa) × 23 × 10½ (11½ full load) feet: one shaft, 6-cyl. Fairbanks Morse diesel engine (bore 14″ × 17″ stroke) B.H.P. 630 = 10 knots, oil fuel: one 3-inch/50cal. gun: complement not known.

Ex-mercantile: **GOLDFINCH**
455 tons: 122½(pp) 132½(oa) × 24 × 9¾ (11 full load) feet: one shaft, 6-cyl. Cooper-Bessemer diesel engine (bore 16″ × 20″ stroke) B.H.P. 510 = 10 knots, oil fuel: one 3-inch/50cal gun: complement not known.

Ex-mercantile: **GOLDCREST(i)**
185 tons: 110½(oa) × 21 × 8½ feet: one shaft, Winton diesel engine B.H.P. 600 = 13 knots, oil fuel: two 3-inch/23cal A.A. (2 × 1), two ·3-inch A.A. (2 × 1) guns: complement not known.

Ex-mercantile: **GOSHAWK**
585 tons: 150(oa) × 25 × 10¼ (12½ full load) feet: one shaft, Nelseco diesel engine B.H.P. 400 = 10 knots, oil fuel: one 3-inch/50cal gun: complement not known.

Ex-mercantile: **GOLDCREST(ii), CHAFFINCH**
400 tons (*Goldcrest*) 410 tons (*Chaffinch*): 115(pp) 122½(oa) × 23 × 11 feet: one shaft, Atlas diesel engine (bore 14¼″ × 21″ stroke) B.H.P. 600 = 11 knots, one 3-inch/50cal gun: complement 36.

Ex-mercantile: **EAGLE**
520 tons: 133½(oa) × 26 × 12¾ (full load) feet: one shaft, 6-cyl. Cooper-Bessemer diesel engine (bore 15½″ × 22″ stroke) B.H.P. 650 = 12½ knots. oil fuel: one 4-inch/50cal, two ·5-inch A.A. (2 × 1) guns: complement 47.

Ex-mercantile: **HAWK, IBIS, MERGANSER**
530 tons: 133¾(pp) 147(oa) × 26 × 13 (full load) feet: one shaft, 6-cyl. Cooper-Bessemer diesel engine (bore 15½″ × 22″ stroke) B.H.P. 650 = 11½ knots, oil fuel: two 6-pounder (2 × 1), two ·5-inch A.A. (2 × 1) guns: complement not known.

Bluebird(i)
(ex-mercantile *Maine*)
Hull No: AM.72

Launched: 7.4.31

Built by: Associated Sbdr. (Seattle)

IX.171 (1944); transferred Maritime Commission 15.11.45 for disposal.

Grackle(i)
(ex-mercantile *Notre Dame*)
Hull No: AM.73

Launched: 1929

Built by: As above

Transferred Maritime Commission 9.9.46 for disposal.

Gull(i)
(ex-mercantile *Hull No:* AM.74

Launched: 1928

Boston College)

Built by: As above

Transferred Maritime Commission 9.9.46 for disposal.

Kite(i)
(ex-mercantile *Holy Cross)*
Hull No: AM.75

Launched: 1928

Built by: As above

Transferred War Shipping Admin. 2.3.45 for disposal

Left: *Auxiliary minesweeper* GRACKLE*(i) (15 Oct 1941) was armed with a 3in/23cal gun forward.*
Above: Auxiliary minesweeper LINNET*(i) (4 Feb 1941): note horizontal LL sweep drum on the poop.*
PHOTOGRAPHS: U.S. NAVY

Linnet(i)
(ex-mercantile
Georgetown)
Hull No: AM.76

Built by: As above

IX.166 (1944), mercantile
Cambridge (1945).

Launched:
1928

Goldfinch(i)

Fordham)
Hull No: AM.77

Built by: As above

Sold Norwegian Shpg &
Trade Commission 9.1.46.

Launched:
1929

Goldcrest(i)
(ex-yacht *Stella
Polaris*,
ex-*Armina*)
Hull No: AM.78

Built by: Mathis Yacht
(Camden)

Agate (PYc.4—1940).

Launched:
1930

Goshawk
(ex-mercantile
Penobscot)
Hull No: AM.79

Built by: Foundation
(Savannah)

IX.195 (1944), mercantile
Bering Sea (1946).

Launched:
1919

Goldcrest(ii)
(ex-mercantile
Shawmut)
Hull No: AM.80

Built by: Bethlehem
(Quincy)

Mercantile *Batavia* (1946).

Launched:
1928

Chaffinch
(ex-mercantile
Trimount)
Hull No: AM.81

Built by: As above

Mercantile *Medan* (1946).

Launched:
1928

Eagle
(ex-mercantile
Wave,
ex-*Harvard*)
Hull No: AM.132

Built by: As above

Captor (PYc.40—1942).

Launched:
1938

Hawk(i)
(ex-mercantile
Gale,
ex-*West Point*)
Hull No: AM.133

Built by: As above

Retroceded 9.44.

Launched:
1937

Ibis
(ex-mercantile
Tide, ex-*Yale*)
Hull No: AM.134

Built by: Bethlehem
(Quincy)

Sold General Foods Corp.
(Boston) 1945.

Launched:
1937

Merganser(i)
(ex-mercantile
Ocean,
ex-*Annapolis*)
Hull No: AM.135

Built by: As above

Mercantile *Ocean* (1945).

Launched:
1937

"Adroit" class:

Adroit, Advent, Annoy, Conflict, Constant, Daring, Dash, Despite, Direct, Dynamic, Effective, Engage, Excel, Exploit, *Fidelity, *Fierce, *Firm, *Force.

Another emergency measure to provide inshore minesweepers was to adapt eighteen steel patrol craft under construction to this role by shipping light wire sweep gear in place of the mortars and racks for depth charges aft. Owing to their narrow hulls and limited deck space they did not prove wholly satisfactory sweepers, and all reverted to patrol craft (PC) in 1944.

DISPLACEMENT: 295 tons (450 tons full load).
DIMENSIONS: 170(wl) 173¾(oa) × 23 × 6 (7½ full load) feet.
MACHINERY: Two shafts; 8-cylinder General Motors diesel engines (bore 9½" × 12" stroke) B.H.P. 1,770 except ALCO diesel engines B.H.P. 1,400 = 17 knots.
BUNKERS AND RADIUS: O.F. 60 tons; 5,000/1,600 miles @ 10/18 knots.
ARMAMENT: One 5-inch/50cal, four 20mm A.A. (4 × 1) guns.
COMPLEMENT: 65.

Adroit (ex-*PC.d586*) Hull No: AM.82 Launched: 21.2.42	*Built by:* Commercial I.W. (Portland) PC.1586 (1944).	**Annoy** (ex-*PC.1588*) Hull No: AM.84 Launched: 6.4.42	*Built by:* As above PC.1588 (1944).	**Constant** (ex-*PC.1590*) Hull No: AM.86 Launched: 9.5.42	*Built by:* As above PC.1590 (1944).
Advent (ex-*PC.1587*) Hull No: AM.83 Launched: 12.3.42	*Built by:* As above PC.1587 (1944).	**Conflict** (ex-*PC.1589*) Hull No: AM.85 Launched: 18.4.42	*Built by:* As above PC.1589 (1944).	**Daring** (ex-*PC.1591*) Hull No: AM.87 Launched: 23.5.42	*Built by:* As above PC.1591 (1944).

Below: The DESPITE *(26 Aug 1942). Right: The* ENGAGE *(23 Oct 1942).*   PHOTOGRAPHS: U.S. NAVY

Dash
(ex-*PC.1592*)
Hull No: AM.88

Built by: As above

PC.1592 (1944).

Launched:
20.6.42

Despite
(ex-*PC.1593*)
Hull No: AM.89

Built by: Dravo Corp.
(Pittsburgh)

PC.1593 (1944).

Launched:
28.3.42

Direct
(ex-*PC.1594*)
Hull No: AM.90

Built by: Dravo Corp.
(Pittsburgh)

PC.1594 (1944).

Launched:
25.4.42

Dynamic
(ex-*PC.1595*)
Hull No: AM.91

Built by: As above

PC.1595 (1944).

Launched:
26.5.42

Effective
(ex-*PC.1596*)
Hull No: AM.92

Built by: As above

PC.1596 (1944).

Launched:
13.6.42

Engage
(ex-*PC.1597*)
Hull No: 93

Built by: Dravo Corp.
(Pittsburg)

PC.1597 (1944).

Launched:
11.7.42

Excel
(ex-*PC.1598*)
Hull No: AM.94

Built by: Jakobson Shyd.
(Oyster Bay)

PC.1598 (1944).

Launched:

Exploit
(ex-*PC.1599*)
Hull No: AM.95

Built by: As above

PC.1599 (1944).

Launched:
7.9.42

Fidelity*
(ex-*PC.1600*)
Hull No: AM.96

Built by: Nashville Bridge

PC.1600 (1944).

Launched:
28.2.42

Fierce*
(ex-*PC.1601*)
Hull No: AM.97

Built by: As above

PC.1601 (1944).

Launched:
5.3.42

Firm*
(ex-*PC.1602*)
Hull No: AM.98

Built by: Penn-Jersey
Sbdg. (Camden)

PC.1602 (1944).

Launched:
29.5.42

Force*
(ex-*PC.1603*)
Hull No: AM.99

Built by: As above

PC. 1603 (1944).

Launched:
7.9.42

Machinery contracts: All engined by Cooper-Bessemer except *last four* by ALCO.

"Admirable" class:

Adjutant, Admirable, Adopt, Advocate, Agent, Alarm, Albatross, Alchemy, Apex, Arcade, Arch, Armada, Aspire, Assail, Astute, Augury, Barrier, Bittern, Bluebird, Bombard, Bond, Breakhorn, Bullfinsh, Buoyant, Candid, Capable, Captivate, Caravan, Cardinal, Cariama, Caution, Change, Chukor, Clamour, Climax, Compel, Concise, Control, Counsel, Crag, Creddock, Cruise, Deft, Delegate, Density, Design, Device, Diploma, Dipper, Disdain, Dotterel, Dour, Drake, Driver, Dunlin, Eager, Elusive, Embattle, Embroil, Enhance, Equity, Esteem, Event, Execute, Facility, Fancy, Firecrest, Fixity, Flame, Flicker, Fortify, Gadwall, Garland, Gavia, Gayety, Goldfinch, Grackle, Graylag, Grosbeak, Grouse, Gull, Harlequin, Harrier, Hawk, Hazard, Hilarity, Hummer(i), Hummer(ii), Illusive, Imbue, Impervious, Implicit, Improve, Inaugural, Incessant, Incredible, Indicative, Inflict, Instill, Intrigue, Invade, Jackdaw(i), Jackdaw(ii), Jubilant, Kite, Knave, Lance, Linnet, Logic, Longspur, Lucid, Magpie, Magnet, Mainstay, Marvel, Measure, Medrick, Merganser, Method, Minah, Mirth, Nimble, Notable, Nucleus, Opponent, Osprey, Palisade, Parakeet, Partridge, Penetrate, Peril, Phantom, Pinnacle, Pipit, Pirate, Pivot, Pledge, Plover, Prime, Project, Prowess, Quest, Rampart, Ransom, Rebel, Recruit, Redhead, Reform, Refresh, Reign, Report, Reproof, Risk, Rival, Sagacity, Salute, Sanderling, Saunter, Scaup, Scout, Scrimmage, Scuffle, Scurry, Sentinel, Sentry, Serene, Shearwater, Shelter, Signet, Skirmish, Spectacle, Specter, Staunch, Strategy, Strength, Success, Superior, Waxbill, and **Two** unnamed.

DISPLACEMENT: 650 tons (945 tons full load).
DIMENSIONS: 180(wl) 184½(oa) × 33 × 8½ (9¾ full load) feet.
MACHINERY: Two shafts; 8-cylinder Cooper-Bessemer (bore 10½″ × 13½″ stroke) except *AM.136–165* ALCO and *AM.351–370* Busch-Sulzer diesel engines B.H.P. 1,710 = 15 (14¾ full load) knots.
BUNKERS AND RADIUS: O.F. 260 tons; 5,600 miles @ 10 knots.
ARMAMENT: One 3-inch/50cal A.A., two 40mm A.A. (2 × 1), two 20mm A.A. (2 × 1) guns.
COMPLEMENT: 104.

The after 3in A.A. has been replaced by two 40mm A.A. (2 × 1) guns in the CARAVAN *(18 Jan 1944) and two extra 20mm A.A. (2 × 1) guns added forward of the bridge.* PHOTOGRAPH: U.S. NAVY

Top left: The ADMIRABLE *(3 June 1943) as completed with 3in A.A. guns forward and aft. Top right: The diesel engine exhausts were led overside in the* AUGURY *(25 Apr 1944), but some units of the class were fitted with a small funnel (vide photograph of the* ADOPT*) or thin exhaust pipe. Lower left: The* ADOPT *(6 June 1944) with augmented light A.A. armament: note that only one boat is carried on the port side abreast the funnel. Lower right: The* GAYETY *(3 Jan 1945).* PHOTOGRAPHS: U.S. NAVY

One solution to meet the numerical demand for minesweepers was to reduce unit size, and in this respect the "Admirable" class can be considered basic sweepers (much the same as the British "Bangor" class) to meet minimum requirements for size, speed and endurance. They were first classed as coastal minesweepers (AMc) but were more appropriately re-rated as minesweepers (AM) prior to laying-down.

Owing to the reduced length of this class the fo'c'sle deck was extended farther aft than with the *Auk* to provide additional berthing, and with their large and high bridge and absence of conventional funnel they always tended to look smaller than they were. Main propulsion reverted to direct diesel drive, with the engines coupled to the shafts though single-reduction gearing, as the most compact arrangement; and the exhausts were led either to a thin smoke pipe or a small and short funnel. Rigging comprised a tall tripod foremost with forward leading legs carrying SW.DRF at its head, while a short mainmast was fitted with the D/F loop. Boats stowed abaft the bridge were handled by derricks stepped from the after side of the foremast.

They were fitted for both wire and LL sweeping; and were armed with a 3in A.A. gun on the fo'c'sle, two 20mm A.A. (2 × 1) guns on the bridge, and two 40mm A.A. (2 × 1) guns at the break of the fo'c'sle; and were equipped with both sonar and depth charges. In later units more twin mountings replaced the single 40mm A.A. guns and four more 20mm A.A. (4 × 1) guns were added; a split spigot A/X mortar (Hedgehog) was installed forward of the bridge; and AW.RDF replaced the SW set at the masthead, with the latter re-positioned slightly lower on the mast.

Of the 180 units authorised, forty eight were cancelled and two completed as mercantile; while in 1945 thirty-four units were transferred to the Soviet Navy. Within their limitations the "Admirable" class proved very satisfactory small minesweepers, and were also frequently employed on patrol and escort duties.

Admirable
Hull No: AM.136

Launched:
18.10.42

Built by: Tampa Sbdg.
Soviet Navy *T.521* (1945); certified unseaworthy 1954 and probably scrapped U.S.S.R.

Adopt
Hull No: AM.137

Launched:
18.10.42

Built by: As above
Soviet Navy *T.522* (1945); scrapped U.S.S.R. probably following war damage.

Advocate
Hull No: AM.138

Launched:
1.11.42

Built by: As above
Soviety Navy *T.111* (1943); destroyed Barents Sea 1956 under U.S.N. supervision.

Agent
Hull No: AM.139

Launched:
1.11.42

Built by: As above
Soviet Navy *T.112* (1943); destroyed Barents Sea 1956 under U.S.N. supervision.

Alarm
Hull No: AM.140

Launched:
7.12.42

Built by: As above
Soviet Navy *T.113* (1943); destroyed Barents Sea 1956 under U.S.N. supervision.

Alchemy
Hull No: AM.141

Launched:
7.12.42

Built by: As above
Soviet Navy *T.114* (1943); torpedoes German submarine *U.365* Kara Sea 12.8.44.

Apex
Hull No: AM.142

Launched:
7.12.42

Built by: As above
Soviet Navy *T.115* (1943); destroyed Barents Sea 1956 under U.S.N. supervision.

Arcade
Hull No: AM.143

Launched:
7.12.42

Built by: As above
Soviet Navy *T.116* (1943); cause, place, and date of loss unknown.

Arch
Hull No: AM.144

Launched:
7.12.42

Built by: Tampa Sbdg.
Soviet Navy *T.117* (1943); scrapped U.S.S.R. post-war probably following war damage.

Armada
Hull No: AM.145

Launched:
7.12.42

Built by: As above
Soviet Navy *T.118* (1943); torpedoed German submarine *U.365* Kara Sea 12.8.44.

The HILARITY *(13 Jan 1945).* PHOTOGRAPH: U.S. NAVY

Aspire
Hull No: AM.146

Launched:
27.12.42

Built by: As above

Soviet Navy *T.119* (1943);
destroyed Barents Sea
1956 under U.S.N.
supervision.

Assail
Hull No: AM.147

Launched:
27.12.42

Built by: As above

Soviet Navy *T.120* (1943);
torpedoed German
submarine *U.739* West
Siberian Sea 24.9.44.

Astute
Hull No: AM.148

Launched:
23.2.43

Built by: As above

Soviet Navy *T.523* (1945);
certified unseaworthy 1954
and probably scrapped
U.S.S.R.

Augury
Hull No: AM.149

Launched:
23.2.43

Built by: As above

Soviet Navy *T.524* (1945);
certified unseaworthy 1954
and probably scrapped
U.S.S.R.

Barrier
Hull No: AM.150

Launched:
23.2.43

Built by: As above

Soviet Navy *T.525* (1945);
certified unseaworthy 1954
and probably scrapped
U.S.S.R.

Bombard
Hull No: AM.151

Launched:
23.2.43

Built by: As above

Soviet Navy *T.526* (1945);
certified unseaworthy 1954
and probably scrapped
U.S.S.R.

Bond
Hull No: AM.152

Launched:
21.10.42

Built by: Williamette Iron
& Steel (Portland)

Soviet Navy *T.593* (1945);
certified unseaworthy 1954
and probably scrapped
U.S.S.R.

Buoyant
Hull No: AM.153

Launched:
24.11.42

Built by: Williamette Iron
& Steel (Portland)

Sold (Shanghai)
29.5.46.

Candid
Hull No: AM.154

Launched:
14.10.42

Built by: As above

Soviet Navy *T.594* (1945);
certified unseaworthy 1954
and probably scrapped
U.S.S.R.

Capable
Hull No: AM.155

Launched:
16.11.42

Built by: As above

Soviet Navy *T.595* (1945);
certified unseaworthy 1954
and probably scrapped
U.S.S.R.

Captivate
Hull No: AM.156

Launched:
1.12.42

Built by: As above

Soviet Navy *T.596* (1945);
certified unseaworthy 1954
and probably scrapped
U.S.S.R.

Caravan
Hull No: AM.157

Launched:
27.10.42

Built by: As above

Soviet Navy *T.597* (1945);
certified unseaworthy 1954
and probably scrapped
U.S.S.R.

Below left: The auxiliary coastal minesweeper PIPIT *(1 Aug 1941). Below right: The auxiliary coastal minesweeper* MAGPIE *(1 Aug 1941). Bottom left: The auxiliary coastal minesweeper* PLOVER *(21 Oct 1941). Bottom right: The auxiliary coastal minesweeper* GROSBEAK *(14 Apr 1941)*   PHOTOGRAPHS: U.S. NAVY

Caution
Hull No: AM.158

Launched:
7.12.42

Built by: As above

Soviet Navy *T.598* (1945);
certified unseaworthy 1954
and probably scrapped
U.S.S.R.

Climax
Hull No: AM.161

Launched:
9.1.43

Built by: As above

MSF.161 (1955); stricken
1.12.59 and scrapped.

Control
Hull No: AM.164

Launched:
28.143

Built by: As above

MSF.164 (1955); sold
30.3.59 and scrapped.

Change
Hull No: AM.159

Launched:
15.12.42

Built by: As above

MSF.159 (1955); stricken
1960 and scrapped.

Compel
Hull No: AM.162

Launched:

Built by: As above

MSF.162 (1955); sold
26.8.60 and scrapped.

Counsel
Hull No: AM.165

Launched:
17.2.43

Built by: As above

MSF.165 (1955); stricken
1.7.72.

Clamour
Hull No: AM.160

Launched:
24.12.42

Built by: As above

MSF.160 (1955); stricken
1.12.59 and scrapped.

Concise
Hull No: AM.163

Launched:
6.2.43

Built by: As above

MSF.163 (1955); stricken
1.12.59 and scrapped.

Top: The auxiliary coastal minesweeper CONDOR *(13 May 1941). Above: The auxiliary coastal
minesweepers* LONGSPUR *(1 Aug 1941) and* WAXBILL *(14 July 1941).*   PHOTOGRAPHS: U.S. NAVY

Unnamed *Hull No:* AM.166–208	*Built by:* unknown Cancelled 9.4.42.	

Unnamed *Hull No:* AM.209–213	*Built by:* unknown Cancelled 10.4.42.

Crag
(ex-*Craig*)
Hull No: AM.214

Launched:
21.3.43

Built by: Tampa Sbdg.
Completed Charleston
N.Y., MSF.214 (1955),
Mexican Navy *DM.15*
(1962).

Cruise
Hull No: AM.215

Launched:
21.3.43

Built by: As above
Completed Charleston
N.Y., MSF.215 (1955);
stricken 1.7.72.

Deft
Hull No: AM.216

Launched:
28.3.43

Built by: As above
Chinese Navy (1948); sold
16.1.59 and scrapped.

Delegate
Hull No: AM.217

Launched:
28.3.43

Built by: Tampa Sbdg.
Chinese Navy
(Nationalist) *Yung Ho*
(1946); scrapped 1964.

Density
Hull No: AM.218

Launched:
6.2.44

Built by: As above
MSF.218 (1955); stricken
1960 and scrapped.

Design
Hull No: AM.219

Launched:
6.2.44

Built by: As above
MSF.219 (1955); stricken
1960 and scrapped.

Device
Hull No: AM.220

Launched:
21.5.44

Built by: As above
MSF.220 (1955), Mexican
Navy *DM.11* (1962).

Diploma
Hull No: AM.221

Launched:
21.5.44

Built by: As above
MSF.221 (1955), Mexican
Navy *DM.17* (1962).

Below left: The auxiliary coastal minesweeper EGRET *(8 July 1941). Below right: The* CHACALACA
(22 Aug 1941) fitting out. Bottom left: The naval-designed CARACARA *(21 Oct 1941) was largely based on
the commercial craft acquired as auxiliary coastal minesweepers: note horizontal reel aft for the LL sweep.
Bottom right: The* AGGRESSOR *(23 Dec 1941): note vertical reel for LL sweep.* PHOTOGRAPHS: U.S. NAVY

Disdain
Hull No: AM.222

Launched:
25.3.44

Built by: American Sbdg. (Lorain)

Soviet Navy *T.277* (1945).

Dour
Hull No: AM.223

Launched:
25.3.44

Built by: As above

MSF.223 (1955), Mexican Navy *DM.16* (1962).

Eager
Hull No: AM.224

Launched:
10.6.44

Built by: As above

MSF.224 (1955), Mexican Navy *DM.06* (1962).

Elusive
Hull No: AM.225

Launched:
10.6.44

Built by: As above

Chinese Navy (Nationalist) *Yung Kang* (1946); scrapped 1964...

Embattle
Hull No: AM.226

Launched:
17.9.44

Built by: American Sbdg. (Lorain)

Chinese Navy (Nationalist) *Yung Hsing* (1946); scrapped 1964.

Embroil
Hull No: AM.227

Built by: As above

Cancelled 6.6.44.

Enhance
Hull No: AM.228

Built by: As above

Cancelled 6.6.44.

Equity
Hull No: AM.229

Built by: As above

Cancelled 6.6.44.

Esteem
Hull No: A 230

Built by: As above

Cancelled 6.6.44.

Event
Hull No: AM.231

Built by: As above

Cancelled 6.6.44.

Execute
Hull No: AM.232

Launched:
22.6.44

Built by: Puget Sound Bridge (Seattle)

MSF.232 (1955), Mexican Navy *DM.03* (1962).

Facility
Hull No: AM.233

Launched:
22.6.44

Built by: As above

MSF.233 (1955), Mexican Navy *DM.04* (1962); scrapped 1971.

Fancy
Hull No: AM.234

Launched:
4.9.44

Built by: As above

Soviet Navy *T.271* (1945).

Fixity
Hull No: AM.235

Launched:
4.9.44

Built by: As above

Mercantile *Commercial Dixie* (1949).

Flame
Hull No: AM.236

Built by: As above

Cancelled 6.6.44.

Fortify
Hull No: AM.237

Built by: As above

Cancelled 6.6.44.

Garland
Hull No: AM.238

Launched:
20.2.44

Built by: Winslow Marine (Seattle)

MSF.238 (1955); sold Ships & Power Inc. (Miami) 24.10.60 and scrapped.

Gayety
Hull No: AM.239

Launched:
19.3.34

Built by: As above

MSF.239 (1955), South Viet-Namese Navy *Chi Lang II* (1962).

Hazard
Hull No: AM.240

Launched:
21.5.44

Built by: As above

MSF.240 (1955); sold Howard Stone (Palm Springs) 22.10.68 and scrapped.

Below: The AVENGE *(21 Mar 1942) on trials. Bottom: The armament of two A.A. (2 × 1) machine guns was shipped on the wheelhouse roof of the* BOLD *(22 May 1942).* PHOTOGRAPHS: U.S. NAVY

Hilarity
Hull No: AM.241

Launched:
30.7.44

Built by: As above

MSF.241 (1955), Mexican Navy *DM.02* (1962).

Inaugural
Hull No: AM.242

Launched:
1.10.44

Built by: As above

MSF.242 (1955); hulk as floating museum St. Louis (1968).

Illusive
Hull No: AM.243

Built by As above

Cancelled 6.6.44 and scrapped on slip.

Imbue
Hull No: AM.244

Built by: As above

Cancelled 6.6.44 and scrapped on slip.

Impervious
Hull No: AM.245

Built by: As above

Cancelled 6.6.44 and scrapped on slip.

Implicit
Hull No: AM.246

Launched:
6.9.43

Built by: Savannah Machine

Chinese Navy (Nationalist) *Yung Chia* (1948).

Improve
Hull No: AM.247

Launched:
26.9.43

Built by: As above

Mercantile *Ecuador* (1949); lost cause and place unknown 16.3.53.

Incessant
Hull No: AM.248

Launched:
22.10.43

Built by: Savannah Machine

Mercantile *Commercial Ohioan* (1949).

Incredible
Hull No: AM.249

Launched:
21.11.43

Built by: As above

MSF.249 (1955); sold National Metal & Steel Corp. 8.8.60 and scrapped.

Indicative
Hull No: AM.250

Launched:
12.12.43

Built by: As above

Soviet Navy *T.728* (1945); lost cause, place and date unknown.

Inflict
Hull No: AM.251

Launched:
16.1.44

Built by: As above

Mercantile *Manabi* (1948); lost cause and place unknown 24.4.53.

Instill
Hull No: AM.252

Launched:
5.3.44

Built by: As above

MSF.252 (1955), Mexican Navy *DM.10* (1962).

Intrigue
Hull No: AM.253

Launched:
8.4.44

Built by: As above

MSF.253 (1955), Mexican Navy *DM.19* (1962).

Invade
Hull No: AM.254

Launched:
2.6.44

Built by: As above

MSF.254 (1955), Mexican Navy *DM.18* (1962).

Jubilant
Hull No: AM.255

Launched:
20.2.43

Built by: American Sbdg. (Lorain)

MSF.255 (1955), Mexican Navy *DM.01* (1962).

Knave
Hull No: AM.256

Launched:
13.3.43

Built by: As above

MSF.256 (1955), Mexican Navy *DM.13* (1962).

Below: A vertical reel for the LL sweep was provided at the stern of the BULWARK *(31 Jan 1942). Bottom: The auxiliary coastal minesweeper* AFFRAY *(4 June 1942) was acquired while building and was armed with two twin A.A. machine guns.* PHOTOGRAPHS: U.S. NAVY

Top: YMS-12 (29 May 1942) belonged to the first series with two small funnels and was armed with one 3in A.A. and two 20mm A.A. (2 × 1) guns. Above: YMS-13 (3 Sept 1942). In all of this series the short bulwark abreast the 20mm gun was hinged and was dropped outboard when cleared for action.
PHOTOGRAPHS: U.S. NAVY

Measure
Hull No: AM.263

Launched:
23.10.43

Built by: As above

Soviet Navy *T.273* (1945).

Lance
Hull No: AM.257

Launched:
10.4.43

Built by: American Sbdg. (Lorain)

Chinese Navy (Nationalist) *Yung Sheng* (1945); scrapped 1968.

Magnet
Hull No: AM.260

Launched:
5.6.43

Built by: As above

Chinese Navy (Nationalist) *Yung Shun* (1945); scrapped 1963.

Method
Hull No: AM.264

Launched:
23.10.43

Built by: As above

Soviet Navy *T.274* (1945).

Logic
Hull No: AM.258

Launched:
10.4.43

Built by: As above

Chinese Navy (Nationalist) *Yung Shun* (1945); scrapped 1968.

Mainstay
Hull No: AM.261

Launched:
31.7.43

Built by: As above

MSF.261 (1955); sold National Metal & Steel Corp. 8.8.60 and scrapped.

Mirth
Hull No: AM.265

Launched:

Built by: As above

Soviet Navy *T.275* (1945).

Lucid
Hull No: AM.259

Launched:
5.6.43

Built by: As above

Chinese Navy (Nationalist) *Yung Ting* (1945), *Yang Ming* (1964).

Marvel
Hull No: AM.262

Launched:
31.7.43

Built by: As above

Soviet Navy *T.272* (1945).

Nimble
Hull No: AM.266

Launched:
24.12.43

Built by: As above

Chinese Navy (Nationalist) (1948); scrapped.

Notable	*Built by:* Gulf Sbdg.				
Hull No: AM.267	(Madisonville)				
Launched: 12.6.43	Chinese Maritime Customs (1946).				

Nucleus	*Built by:* As above	**Penetrate**	*Built by:* As above	**Pinnacle**	*Built by:* As above
Hull No: AM.268		Hull No: AM.271		Hqll No: AM.274	
	Soviet Navy T.276 (1945).		Soviet Navy T.280 (1945).		Chinese Navy (Nationalist) *Yung Hsiu* (1948).
Launched: 26.6.43		Launched: 11.9.43		Launched. 11.9.43	

Opponent	*Built by:* As above	**Peril**	*Built by:* As above	**Pirate**	*Built by:* As above
Hull No: AM.269		Hull No: AM.272		Hull No: AM.275	
	MSF.269 (1955); sold Ship & Power Inc. (Miami) 3.2.61.		Soviet Navy T.281 (1945); certified unseaworthy 1954 and probably scrapped U.S.S.R.		Mined off Wonsan 12.10.50.
Launched: 12.6.43		Launched: 25.7.43		Launched: 16.12.43	

Palisade	*Built by:* As above	**Phantom**	*Built by:* As above	**Pivot**	*Built by:* As above
Hull No: AM.270		Hull No: AM.272		Hull No: AM.276	
	Soviet Navy T.279 (1945); mined off Kham Island 14.8.45 and written-off as constructive total loss.		Chinese Navy (Nationalist) *Yung Ming* (1948); scrapped 7.51.		Chinese Navy (Nationalist) *Yung Shou* (1948); scrapped 1968.
Launched: 26.6.43		Launched: 25.7.43		Launched: 11.11.43	

Pledge
Hull No: AM.277

Launched:
23.12.43

Built by: Gulf Sbdg.
(Madisonville)

Mined off Wonsan
12.10.50.

Project
Hull No: AM.278

Launched:
22.1.44

Built by: As above

Philippino Navy Samar
(1948).

Prime
Hull No: AM.279

La.nched:
22.1.44

Built by: As above

Chinese Navy
(Nationalist) Yung Feng
(1946).

Prowess
Hull No: AM.280

Launched:
17.2.44

Built by: As above

MSF.280 (1955), IX.305
(1966), South Viet-
Namese Navy Ho Hoi
(1970).

Quest
Hull No: AM.281

Launched:
16.3.44

Built by: As above

Philippino Navy Apo
(later), Pagasa (1948),
Santa Maria (1955),
Pagasa (later renamed),
Mount Samot (1970).

Rampart
Hull No: AM.282

Launched:
30.3.44

Built by: As above

Soviet Navy T.282 (1945).

Ransom
Hull No: AM.283

Launched:
18.9.43

Built by: General Eng.
(Alameda)

MSF.283 (1955), Mexican
Navy DM.12 (1962).

Rebel
Hull No: AM.284

Launched:
28.10.43

Built by: As above

MSF.284 (1955), Mexican
NavI DM.14 (1962).

Recruit
Hull No: AM.285

Launched:
11.12.43

Built by. As above

MSF.285 (1955), Mexican
Navy DM.07 (1962);
scrapped 1971.

Reform
Hull No: AM.286

Launched:
29.1.44

Built by: As above

Refresh
Hull No: AM.287

Launched:
12.4.44

Built by: General Eng.
(Alameda)

Chinese Navy
(Nationalist) Yung Chang
(1948); gunfire Chinese
Navy (Communist)
gunboats off Southern
China 14.11.65.

Reign
Hull No: AM.288

Launched:
29.5.44

Built by: As above

MSF.288 (1955); stricken
1.12.59 and scrapped.

Report
Hull No: AM.289

Launched:
8.7.44

Built by: As above

MSF.289 (1955), U.S.
Army (name unchanged—
1963), South Korean Navy
Kojin.

Reproof
Hull No: AM.290

Launched:
8.8.44

Built by: As above

Completed mercantile
Harcourt Matcolm (1947),
Colton Bay (1953),
Stratford (1960).

Risk
Hull No: AM.291

Launched:
7.11.44

Built by: As above

Completed mercantile
George Gamblin (1947),
Winding Bay (1953),
Pinguino (1963).

Rival
Hull No: AM.292

Built by: As above

Cancelled 6.6.64.

Sagacity
Hull No: AM.293

Built by: As above

Cancelled 6.6.44.

Salute
Hull No: AM.294

Launched:
6.2.43

Built by: Winslow Marine
(Seattle)

Mined off Brunei 8.6.45.

Saunter
Hull No: AM.295

Launched:
20.2.43

Built by: As above

Sold 4.47 and scrapped.

Scout
Hull No: AM.296

Launched:
2.5.43

Built by: Winslow Marine
(Seattle)

MSF.296 (1955), Mexican
Navy DM.09 (1962);
scrapped 1971.

BYMS-2189 (ex-YMS-189) paid-off and awaiting disposal.   PHOTOGRAPH: P. A. VICARY

Scrimmage
Hull No: AM.297

Launched:
16.5.43

Built by: As above

MSF.297 (1955),
mercantile *Giant II* (1962).

Scuffle
Hull No: AM.298

Launched:
8.8.43

Built by: As above

MSF.298 (1955), Mexican
Navy *DM.05* (1962).

Sentry
Hull No: AM.299

Launched:
15.8.43

Built by: As above

MSF.299 (1955), South
Viet-Namese Navy *Ky Hoa*
(1962).

Serene
Hull No: AM.300

Launched:
31.10.43

Built by: As above

MSF.300 (1955), South
Viet-Namese Navy *Nhut
Tao* (1964).

Shelter
Hull No: AM.301

Launched:
14.11.43

Built by: As above

MSF.301 (1955), South
Viet-Namese *Chi Linh*
(1964).

Signet
Hull No: AM.302

Launched:
16.8.43

Built by: Associated Sbds.
(Seattle)

MSF.302 (1955),
Dominican Navy
Separacion (1965).

Skirmish
Hull No: AM.303

Launched:
16.8.43

Built by: As above

MSF.303 (1955),
Dominican Navy
Tortugero (1965).

Scurry
(ex-*Skurry*)
Hull No: AM.304

Launched:
1.10.43

Built by: As above

MSF.304 (1955); stricken
1.5.67 and scrapped.

Spectacle
Hull N. AM.305

Launched:
1.10.43

Built by: Associated Sbds.
(Seattle)

Sold 5.47 and scrapped.

Specter
(ex-*Spector*)
Hull No: AM.306

Launched:
15.2.44

Built by: As above

MSF.306 (1955); stricken
1.7.72.

Top: YMS–446 (30 June 1944) was the lead ship of the third series which were ex-PCS conversions re-adapted for minesweeping, and retained the PCS features of a larger bridge and no funnel. Above: As the diesel exhausts were led overside no funnel was fitted in YMS 453 (8 July 1944). PHOTOGRAPHS: U.S. NAVY

Staunch
Hull No: AM.307

Launched:
15.2.44

Built by: As above

MSF.307 (1955); stricken
1.4.67 and scrapped.

Strength
Hull No: AM.309

Launched:
28.3.44

Built by: As above

MSF.309 (1955), hulked
for salvage training (1968).

Strategy
Hull No: AM.308

Launched:
28.3.44

Built by: As above

MSF.308 (1955);
sold, arrived Portsmouth
(Va) 1969 and scrapped.

Success
Hull No: AM.310

Launched:
11.5.44

Built by: As above

MSF.310 (1955), Mexican
Navy *DM.08* (1962);
scrapped 1971.

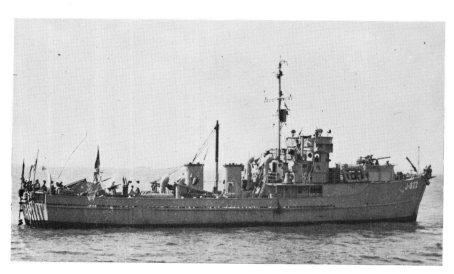

Top: **BYMS-2022** in British service in 1943. Above: **PCE-867** (27 May 1943) was an Admirable class hull adapted for escort work, and was armed with two 3in A.A. (2×1) and three 20mm A.A. (3×1) guns.
PHOTOGRAPHS: P. A. VICARY and U.S. NAVY

Superior
Hull No: AM.311

Launched:
11.5.44

Built by: As above

MSF.311 (1955); stricken 1.7.72.

Unnamed
Hull No: AM.312

Built by: As above

Cancelled 7.5.42.

Unnamed
Hull No: AM.313

Built by: As above

Cancelled 7.5.42.

Unnamed
Hull No:
AM.342–350

Built by: unknown

Hull numbers not used.

Adjutant
Hull No: AM.351

Launched:
17.6.44

Built by: Williamette Iron & Steel (Portland)

Cancelled 1.11.45 and scrapped incomplete.

Bittern(ii)
Hull No: AM.352

Launched:
21.6.44

Built by: As above

Cancelled 1.11.45 and scrapped incomplete.

Breakdown
Hull No: AM.353

Launched:
4.7.44

Built by: As above

Cancelled 1.11.45 and scrapped incomplete.

Cariama
Hull No: AM.354

Launched:
1.7.44

Built by: As above

Cancelled 1.11.45 and scrapped incomplete.

Chukor
Hull No: AM.355

Launched:
15.7.44

Built by: As above

Cancelled 1.11.45 and scrapped incpmplete.

Creddock
Hull No: AM.356

Launched:
22.7.44

Built by: As above

MSF.356 (1955), Burmese Navy *Yan Gyi Aung* (1967).

Dipper
Hull No: AM.357

Launched:
26.7.44

Built by: As above

MSF.357 (1955); sold 5.1.61 and scrapped.

Dotterel
Hull No: AM.358

Launched:
5.8.44

Built by: As above

Cancelled 11.11.45 and scrapped incomplete.

Drake
Hull No: AM.359

Launched:
12.8.44

Built by: As above

Completed *Ampere* (YDG.11), ADG.11 (1955); stricken 1.7.61 and scrapped.

Driver
Hull No: AM.360

Launched:
19.8.44

Built by: As above

Cancelled 1.11.45 and scrapped incomplete.

Dunlin
Hull No: AM.361

Launched:
26.8.43

Built by: Williamette Iron & Steel (Portland)

Gadwall
Hull No: AM.362

Launched:
15.7.43

Built by: As above

MSF.362 (1955); mercantile (1968).

Gavia
(ex-*PCE:907*)
Hull No: AM.363

Launched:
18.9.43

Built by: As above

Chinese Navy (Nationalist) *Yung Chun* (1946); scrapped 1964.

Graylag
Hull No: AM.364

Launched:
4.12.43

Built by: As above

MSF.364 (1955); stricken 1.10.67 and scrapped.

Harlequin
Hull No: AM.365

Launched:
3.6.44

Built by: As above

MSF.365 (1955), Mexican Navy *DM.20* (1962).

Harrier
Hull No: AM.366

Launched:
7.6.44

Built by: As above

MSF.366 (1955); stricken 1.12.59 and scrapped.

Below: PCE-831 (11 Sept 1943) running trials with armament not yet shipped. A 40mm A.A. has replaced the 20mm A.A. gun at the stern. Bottom: In PCE-873 (20 Aug 1944) two more 20mm A.A. (2 × 1) guns have been added forward of the bridge, and the after 3in A.A. replaced by two 40mm A.A. (2 × 1) guns.
PHOTOGRAPHS: U.S. NAVY

Top: As shown in PCE-893 (9 Aug 1944) a fifth 20mm A.A. was later added on the starboard side abaft the bridge and only one boat was carried on the port side. Above: PCE(R)-856 (30 Nov 1944) was modified for rescue work with the fo'c'sle extended well aft. Boats were deck-stowed on each side of the funnel and the amidships 20mm A.A. gun was moved farther aft and paired with an extra gun on the port side.
PHOTOGRAPHS: U.S. NAVY

Hummer(i)	*Built by:* Puget Sound	**Medrick(i)**	*Built by:* As above	**Bullfinch(ii)**	*Built by:* As above
Hull No: AM.367	Bridge (Seattle)	*Hull No:* AM.369		*Hull No:* AM.392	
			Cancelled 6.6.44.		Cancelled 1.11.45 and
Launched:	Cancelled 6.6.44.				scrapped on slip.

Hummer(i)
Hull No: AM.367
Launched:

Built by: Puget Sound Bridge (Seattle)
Cancelled 6.6.44.

Jackdaw(i)
Hull No: AM.368
Built by: As above
Cancelled 6.6.44.

Medrick(i)
Hull No: AM.369
Built by: As above
Cancelled 6.6.44.

Minah(i)
Hull No: AM.370
Built by: As above
Cancelled 6.6.44.

Albatross(ii)
Hull No: AM.391
Built by: Defoe Sbdg. (Bay City)
Cancelled 1.11.45.

Bullfinch(ii)
Hull No: AM.392
Built by: As above
Cancelled 1.11.45 and scrapped on slip.

Cardinal(ii)
Hull No: AM.393
Built by: As above
Cancelled 1.11.45 and scrapped on slip.

Firecrest(ii)
Hull No: AM.394
Built by: As above
Cancelled 1.11.45.

Goldfinch(ii)
Hull No: AM.395
Built by: As above
Cancelled 1.11.45.

Grackle(ii)
Hull No: AM.396
Built by: As above
Cancelled 12.8.45.

Grossbeak(ii)
Hull No: AM.397
Built by: As above
Cancelled 12.8.45.

Grouse(ii)
Hull No: AM.398
Built by: As above
Cancelled 12.8.45.

Gull(ii)
Hull No: AM.399
Built by: As above
Cancelled 12.8.45.

Hawk(ii)
Hull No: AM.400
Built by: As above
Cancelled 12.8.45.

Hummer(ii)
Hull No: AM.401

Built by: As above

Cancelled 12.8.45.

Jackdaw(ii)
Hull No: AM.402

Built by: As above

Cancelled 12.8.45.

Kite(ii)
Hull No: AM.403

Built by: As above

Cancelled 12.8.45.

Longspur(ii)
Hull No: AM.404

Built by: Defoe Sbdg.
(Bay City)

Cancelled 12.8.45.

Merganser(ii)
Hull No: AM.405

Built by: As above

Cancelled 12.8.45.

Osprey(ii)
Hull No: AM.406

Built by: As above

Cancelled 12.8.45.

Partridge(ii)
Hull No: AM.407

Built by: As above

Cancelled 12.8.45.

Plover(ii)
Hull No: AM.408

Built by: As above

Cancelled 12.8.45.

Redhead
Hull No: AM.409

Built by: As above

Cancelled 12.8.45.

Sanderling(ii)
Hull No: AM.410

Built by: As above

Cancelled 12.8.45.

Scaup
Hull No: AM.411

Built by : As above

Cancelled 12.8.45.

Sentinel(ii)
Hull No: AM.412

Built by: As above

Cancelled 12.8.45.

Shearwater
Hull No: AM.413

Built by: As above

Cancelled 12.8.45.

Waxbill(ii)
Hull No: AM.414

Built by: As above

Cancelled 12.8.45.

Top: PCE(R)-855 *was modified in the same way as* PCE(R)-856. *Above:* PCE(C)-899 *was fitted for control duties and had a small deckhouse in place of the 20mm A.A. gun on the starboard side abaft the bridge.*
PHOTOGRAPHS: U.S. NAVY

Bluebird(ii)
Hull No: AM.415

Built by: As above

Cancelled 12.8.45.

Flicker(ii)
Hull No: AM.416

Built by: As above

Cancelled 12.8.45.

Linnet(ii)
Hull No: AM.417

Built by: Defoe Sbdg.
(Bay City)

Cancelled 12.8.45.

Magpie(ii)
Hull No: AM.418

Built by: As above

Cancelled 12.8.45.

Parrakeet(ii)
Hull No: AM.419

Built by: As above

Cancelled 12.8.45.

Pipit(ii)
Hull No: AM.420

Built by: As above

Cancelled 12.8.45.

Machinery contracts: All engined by Cooper-Bessemer except *AM.136–165* ALCO and *AM.351–370* Busch-Sulzer.

"Algerine" class:

These vessels were ordered by the United States Navy from Canada to the standard British fleet minesweeper design, and only differed by mounting two 3-in- A.A. guns forward and aft. By the time their construction was advanced the immediate crisis had passed, and as a result they were all turned over to the Royal Navy: nine under Lend/Lease (AM.325–331, 334, 335), while the contracts for the remaining six (AM.332, 333, 336–339) were terminated by the United States Navy and taken over by the Royal Navy.

Below: PCS-1380 (20 Apr 1945) was a YMS hull adapted for coastal escort work, with the sweep gear aft replaced by a 40mm A.A. and mortars and racks for depth charges. The funnel was eliminated by leading the diesel exhausts overside, and the bridge structure enlarged. Bottom: In PCS-1397 (4 May 1944) two extra 20mm A.A. (2 × 1) guns were added aft in place of A/S mortars: the forward gun to port and the after one to starboard. PHOTOGRAPHS: U.S. NAVY

Unnamed Hull No: AM.325	R.N. *Antares* (1943); returned U.S.N. 12.46.	Unnamed Hull No: AM.330	R.N. *Gozo* (1943), R.H.N. *Polemistis* (1947).	Unnamed Hull No: AM.335	R.N. *Postillion* (1943), R.H.N. *Machitis* (1947).
Unnamed Hull No: AM.326	R.N. *Arcturus* (1943), R.H.N. *Pyrpolitis* (1947)	Unnamed Hull No: AM.331	R.N. *Lightfoot* (1943), R.H.N. *Navamachos* (1947).	Unnamed Hull No: AM.336	R.N. *Solebay* (1942), *Skipjack* (1943).
Unnamed Hull No: AM.327	R.N. *Aries* (1943), R.H.N. *Armatolos* (1946).	Unnamed Hull No: AM.332	R.N. *Melita* (1943).	Unnamed Hull No: AM.337	R.N. *Thisbe* (1943).
Unnamed Hull No: AM.328	R.N. *Clinton* (1943); returned U.S.N. 12.46.	Unnamed Hull No: AM.333	R.N. *Octavia* (1943).	Unnamed Hull No: AM.338	R.N. *Truelove* (1943).
Unnamed Hull No: AM.329	R.N. *Friendship* (1943); returned U.S.N. 12.46	Unnamed Hull No: AM.334	R.N. *Persian* (1943), R.H.N. *Kikiades* (1947).	Unnamed Hull No: AM.339	R.N. *Welfare* (1943).

Top: Rocket projectors have been fitted forward in PCS-1424 *(24 Nov 1943). Above:* PCS-1457 *(21 Feb 1944) had two extra 20mm A.A. (2 × 1) guns aft in place of A/S mortars.*   PHOTOGRAPHS: U.S. NAVY

Decoy Ships

The much-publicised accounts of decoy ship actions during the First World War (when they enjoyed a moderate degree of success) probably resulted in their value being over-estimated. They were again employed by the Royal Navy and the United States Navy in the Second World War, but with singular lack of success as German submarines were more inclined to use the torpedo rather than engage in a surface gun action.

The United States Navy converted six merchant vessels (three elderly cargo steamers, a modern tanker, a trawler, and a 3-masted auxiliary schooner) into decoy ships and concealed their identities under a variety of hull numbers except that no number was ever assigned to the *Atik*. Their entry into service during 1942 was not exactly auspicious: on their first voyages the *Atik* was torpedoed by a German submarine, while the *Irene Forsyte* nearly foundered in heavy weather and was promptly paid-off. The other four all operated until 1943–44 but without success, with an interesting tactical formation comprising the *Big Horn* working in conjunction with two steel patrol craft.

The *Anacapa*, *Asterion*, and *Big Horn* were subsequently employed as weather observing ships, and—except for the *Asterion*—briefly resumed their cargo roles before they were returned to commercial ownership; while the *Captor* saw no further service and was paid-off.

Ex-mercantile: **ASTERION, ATIK**
3,628 tons: 313½(pp) 328¼(oa) × 46 × 25½d/21¼ feet: two SE cylindrical boilers (180lb/in²), one shaft, reciprocating (VTE—cyl. 22″: 37″: 60″ × 42″ stroke) (I.H.P. not known) 11 knots, oil fuel: four 4-inch/50cal (4 × 1), four ·5-inch A.A. (4 × 1) guns: complement 141.

Ex-mercantile: **BIG HORN**
4,150 tons: 425(pp) 441(oa) × 64¼ × 34d/27¾ feet: two w.t. boilers (450lb/in²), one shaft, Westinghouse DR geared turbines (S.H.P. not known) 12½ knots, oil fuel: two 3-inch/50cal (2 × 1) guns: complement 239.

Ex-mercantile: **CAPTOR**
For details see under auxiliary minesweepers and armed yachts.

Ex-mercantile: **IRENE FORSYTE**
285 tons *gross*: 125¼(pp) 144(oa) × 27½ × 11½d/8½ feet: one shaft, 6-cyl. Fairbanks Morse engine (bore 8½″ × 10½″ stroke) B.H.P. 270 = 13 knots, oil fuel: one 4-inch/50cal, one 40mm A.A., two 20mm A.A. (2 × 1) guns: complement not known: wood hull and rigged as 3-masted schooner.

Ex-mercantile: **ANACAPA**
3,321 tons *gross*: 321½(pp) 353(oa) × 50 × 24½d/20½ feet: two SE cylindrical boilers, one shaft, reciprocating (VTE—cyl. 19½″: 31½″: 54½″ × 36″ stroke) (I.H.P. not known) 8 knots, oil fuel: two 4-inch/50cal (2 × 1), two 3-inch/50cal (2 × 1) guns: complement 102.

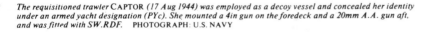

The requisitioned trawler CAPTOR *(17 Aug 1944) was employed as a decoy vessel and concealed her identity under an armed yacht designation (PYc). She mounted a 4in gun on the foredeck and a 20mm A.A. gun aft, and was fitted with SW.RDF.* PHOTOGRAPH: U.S. NAVY

Atik (ex-mercantile *Carolyn*)	*Built by:* Newport News
	Torpedoed German submarine *U.123* 300m east of Norfolk 27.3.42.
Launched: 7.12	
Asterion (ex-mercantile *Evelyn*) Hull No: AK.63	*Built by:* As above
	U.S.C.G. (WAK.123—1944); sold Boston Metals (Baltimore) . . .4.46 and scrapped.
Launched: 6.12	
Big Horn (ex-mercantile *Gulfdawn*) Hull No: AO.45	*Built by:* Sun Sbdg. (Chester)
	U.S.C.G. (WAO.124—1944), U.S.N. (IX.207—1945), mercantile *C. B. Watson* (1947).
Launched: 1936	
Captor (ex-*Eagle*, ex-mercantile *Wave*, ex-*Harvard*) Hull No: PYc.40	*Built by:* Bethlehem (Quincy)
	Transferred War Shpg. Admin. 21/2/45 and sold.
Launched: 1938	
Irene Forsyte (ex-mercantile *Irene Myrtle*, ex-*McLean Clan*) Hull No: IX.93	*Built by:* McLean Con. (Mahone)
	Sold 18.10.45.
Launched: 1920	
Anacapa (ex-mercantile *Coos Bay*, ex-*Lumbertown*, ex-*Castle Town*) Hull No: AG.49	*Built by:* Pusey & Jone (Gloucester City)
	Mercantile *George Olson* (1947).
Launched: 5.19	

Machinery contracts: Big Horn engined by Westinghouse, *Captor* by Cooper-Bessemer, *Irene Forsyte* by Fairbanks Morse, and others by builders.